Raising the
Red Banner

RAISING THE RED BANNER

A PICTORIAL HISTORY OF STALIN'S FLEET
1920–1945

by

Vladimir Yakubov
and Richard Worth

SPELLMOUNT

Unless otherwise credited, all photographs courtesy of
the Boris Lemachko Collection (lemachko@mtu-net.ru)

British Library Cataloguing in Publication Data:
A catalogue record for this book is available
from the British Library

First published 2008

Spellmount Limited
Cirencester Road
Chalford, Stroud
Gloucestershire
GL6 8PE
www.spellmount.com

Spellmount Limited is an imprint of NPI Media Group

1 3 5 7 9 8 6 4 2

Typesetting and origination by NPI Media Group
Printed in Great Britain

Contents

Introduction

In the wake of the Revolution, the reflex to reestablish Russia's traditional naval might ran counter to a host of realities – economic, political, and industrial hurdles that had no immediate solution. The time of rebuilding dragged out over the course of decades while national leaders sought a coherent policy that matched perceived needs to extant capabilities. Their decisions ranged from inspired common sense to self-mutilating fantasy.

Some of the problems came from within. The sailors of the fleet squandered their allowance of Bolshevik good will by ignoring the fact that the time for rebellion had ended. The result was an administrative disaster as the navy became nothing more than an appendage of the army.

While the new government was busy manhandling its constituents, it also succeeded in offending much of the international community, and the first naval diplomacy consisted mostly of losing claim to various Russian vessels lingering overseas. The death of the Tsar's fleet left the Soviets heir to a dubious set of naval assets – the damaged, the disused, and the incomplete – largely disparate except in their shared obsolescence. Wisdom dictated a campaign of scrapping that peaked about 1922. Then followed a modest plan for rehabilitating the healthiest ships, completing the more promising units still in the works, and eventually, some new construction.

Unfortunately, this and subsequent programs would find themselves repeatedly running into Russia's industrial morbidity and getting mashed in the gears of Soviet administration (a term which may be taken to include Stalin's unsubtle personnel policies).

Close on the heels of the purges, the Germans came to impose their own vision on the Soviet navy. Politicized debate on strategic doctrine fell by the way as the country struggled to survive. Among the strengths arising from this crisis was a navy admirably suited to its role as the army's seaward assistant

Building the battleship Imperator Nikolay I. *Launched in 1916, she received little attention thereafter except to be renamed* Demokratiya. *She came through the Civil War largely uninjured but nonetheless subject to rust and obsolescence. The scrapping process came to a close in 1928.*

In wartime, the Soviets found themselves resorting to elaborate camouflage that went well beyond paint schemes. – courtesy of Arseny Malov.

– battleships delivering thunderous artillery support, cruisers and destroyers providing fast transport, and coastal craft performing and countering flank maneuvers.

Given the low estate of the interwar navy and the lack of high-seas glory for the wartime fleet, Soviet warships of this period have failed to emerge from behind the Iron Curtain to gain attention of naval enthusiasts. Yet this period saw the foundation of a fleet that became the "Threat" occupying Western admirals through the decades of the Cold War.

CHAPTER 1

Battleships

The last years of tsarist rule saw an increased acceptance of the navy's dreadnought ambitions. In 1914, the Baltic fleet commissioned four *Sevastopol*-class battleships, and work continued on four *Izmail*-class battlecruisers. In the Black Sea, three battleships of the *Imperatritsa Maria* class were nearing completion; another battleship, *Imperator Nikolay I*, was authorized. Planners looked ahead to battleships carrying 16-inch guns, with construction starting in 1915 and, by 1929 totaling twenty-seven of these super-dreadnoughts and eight battlecruisers.

The Revolution, though, overturned all construction plans, and the industrial base that emerged from civil war could not possibly master the demands of a dreadnought program. The naval establishment saw these practical matters as a temporary set of hurdles and continued its infatuation with theories of big-gun warfare, but adherents to the "Young School" among junior officers saw a counter for brawny battleships in the daring movements of torpedo craft – a concept that took on Marxist connotations. Thus began the enduring pollution of Soviet naval thought by political dogma.

Battleship advocates figured prominently among the early victims of Stalin's personnel moves. For the Young School officers who found themselves rapidly advancing to high-level command, this confirmed the rightness of their cause. In fact, Stalin was simply pruning the tree from the top down, and the upstarts had not yet risen high enough to meet the blade. Their time came soon enough. Ultimately Stalin revealed his true feelings by calling for battleship construction as soon as it became practical – or rather sooner than that.

What Stalin's decision could not do was to assign a distinct role to a Russian battleship. The Soviets lacked facilities for maintaining a battle fleet in the Far East and in the North, while the enclosed waters in other sectors offered little hospitality to capital ships. In the end, it appears the driving force behind

Soviet battleship programs came not from strategic need, but from the lure of prestige.

SEVASTOPOL class

Ship	Builder	Laid Down	Launched	Completed
Sevastopol (ex-*Parizhskaya Kommuna,* ex-*Sevastopol*)	Baltic Works, St. Petersburg	16 Jun 09	10 Jul 11	30 Nov 14
Oktyabr'skaya Revolyutsiya (ex-*Gangut*)	Admiralty Works, St. Petersburg	16 Jun 09	20 Oct 11	11 Jan 15
Frunze (ex-*Poltava*)	Admiralty Works, St. Petersburg	16 Jun 09	23 Jul 11	30 Dec 14
Petropavlovsk (ex-*Marat,* ex-*Petropavlovsk*)	Baltic Works, St. Petersburg	16 Jun 09	22 Sep 11	5 Jan 15

Characteristics (Sevastopol 1944): 30,050 tons full, 184.85 oa x 32.5 x 9.02m, 23.12 knots, 4500nm at 11 knots, twelve 305mm/52, sixteen 120mm/50, six 76mm/55, sixteen 37mm/67, twelve 12.7mm mgs, 1279 men
Characteristics (Marat 1941): 26,184 tons full, 184.00 oa x 26.9 x 8.62m, 22.9 knots, 2310nm at 14 knots, twelve 305mm/52, fourteen 120mm/50, ten 76mm/55, six 37mm/67, thirteen 12.7mm mgs, four 450mm torpedo tubes, 1286 men
Characteristics (Oktyabr'skaya Revolyutsiya 1944): 26,692 tons, 184.85 oa x 26.9 x 9.5m, 22.5 knots, 2700nm at 14 knots, twelve 305mm/52, ten 120mm/50, twelve 76mm/55, twenty 37mm/67, sixteen 12.7mm mgs, four 450mm torpedo tubes, 1411 men

As with all warship designs, the *Sevastopol*s represented a blend of strengths and compromise. By battleship standards, they showed good speed, but the requirement for icebreaking contributed to wet bows and a resulting series of modifications. While the ships entered service with the simplest of silhouettes (an elegant outcome of the quest for minimized target area), in time they sprouted a profusion of modern electronics and fire-control gear.

Sadly, the design's most distinctive characteristic may have been its vulnerability. Designers gave little thought to the danger of torpedoes. Deck protection was scanty and ill placed. The belt armor lacked concentration – a legacy of the Russo-Japanese War.

Among the many misfortunes arising from that conflict, a false lesson wormed its way into Russian thinking. Since the losses at Tsushima had resulted largely from shells that failed to penetrate armor but instead caused damage and fires via explosion, the breadth of armor coverage seemed more important than its thickness. Designers consequently spread the *Sevastopol* armor thinly over almost the entire side area. This armor theory gained acceptance just as new ordnance advances produced shells with considerable armor-piercing ability, saddling the *Sevastopol*s with an armor scheme that became obsolete as they were entering service.

The irony here is that the Russians themselves stood at the forefront of ordnance development. The surviving records of armor trials indicate that their naval shells combined superior armor-piercing caps, reliable TNT bursters, and perhaps a practical delay fuse. While these factors emerged too late for a redesign of the armor scheme, they did serve to give the *Sevastopol*s commendable firepower. The Russian 305mm/52 gun may have been the best 12-inch gun of the First World War.

The triple mounts proved adequate, and though modern critics sometimes bemoan the restricted arcs of the midships mounts, those positions were selected largely to *widen* the firing arcs; turret design at that time lacked adequate blast protection, limiting the use of super-firing mounts.

The Revolution showed no mercy to the Tsar's battleships, and only the *Sevastopol* class survived. For all of their problems, they provided the Reds with the strongest battle fleet of any Baltic nation. Circumstances, though, effectively capped the strategic implications. Independence for Finland and the Baltic States had left the Soviet coastline withered to a meager stretch at the tip of the Gulf of Finland. Stalin managed to recover much of the lost territory, but too late; the events of 1941 erased these gains, and with them, any remaining significance the *Sevastopol*s had as Sea Command assets.

Each ship took a unique path into the Soviet period, but all fell prey to the process of political renaming that would plague Soviet ships for years to come. *Sevastopol* became *Parizhskaya Kommuna* in March 1921 in order to erase any memories of her participation in the anti-Bolshevik revolt in Kronshtadt earlier that month. She transferred to the Black Sea in 1929, which made her the most powerful ship in that sector.

The Soviets treated her to an elaborate upgrade during 1936-39 with improved gun mounts, new deck armor, and hull bulges. Nevertheless, as with the Baltic ships, she had little impact in World War II, her value sapped by the rapid loss of port facilities and the threat of modern aircraft. She performed gamely as an artillery platform and as an armored transport into besieged Sevastopol, and she regained the name *Sevastopol* in 1943.

Like her sister-ship, *Petropavlovsk* received a new name because of her participation in the Kronshtadt revolt. She served as *Marat* until regaining her original name in 1943, at which point she was little more than a wreck; bomb

Parizhskaya Kommuna *(right) and* Marat *in 1924, showing their clean, minimalist profiles – an outcome of the traumatic experience at Tsushima where the large superstructures of the Russian pre-dreadnoughts became pyres under Japanese high-explosive shells.*

damage in 1941 left her only partly afloat, but with three of her turrets still serviceable for bombardment duty. Desperation to preserve her from further damage led to a rather unusual addition to her deck protection – a layer of granite slabs.

A lack of crewmen forced *Gangut* into temporary retirement in 1918, and she returned to duty only in 1925 under the name *Oktyabr'skaya Revolyutsiya*. As with *Parizhskaya Kommuna*, she was modernized in the late 1930s, though not as extensively. She and *Marat* spent the war stuck in Kronshtadt, which gave them the opportunity to torment the Germans with more than 3000 rounds of heavy artillery fire and to guard their sector with relatively powerful anti-aircraft batteries.

Poltava left service at the same time, but neglect and a serious fire ruined her chances for reactivation. Nevertheless, she became *Frunze* in 1926, lingering as a hulk and source of spare parts. Some thought went to using her bow to repair ruined *Marat* until the pair's obvious antiquity killed the plan.

Petropavlovsk in Kronshtadt, 1922, with the results of the Kronshtadt uprising still visible. The aftermath of Revolution left the fleet with a diminished ability to heal its wounds, and the uprising left the government wondering whether those wounds deserved healing.

Oktyabr'skaya Revolyutsiya in 1928 with a few visible changes. She has 76mm Lender AA guns on the forward and aft turrets and open rangefinders atop the conning towers.

Coal-burning battleships steam in line. Note details of the deck planking and the ladders stowed at casemate level. The armored cupola for the 120mm battery commander protrudes just above the casemated guns.

Above and opposite above: *Two views of* Marat *in Kronshtadt. The silhouette, unchanged from Great War views other than the canvas covers on the bridge railings, dates these photos to before the 1928 modernization.*

Below: Parizhskaya Kommuna *in drydock, 1924. Her fore funnel has been altered to reduce the smoke interference with the bridge. This aft view shows the auxiliary anchors and aft conning tower.*

Parizhskaya Kommuna *has her catapult but not the more extensive changes she later received. The German Heinkel K-3 catapult, along with the KR-1 seaplane, was purchased in the 1929. The ship's 1940 modernization removed the catapult to make room for more anti-aircraft armament.*

Shipboard view showing the expanse of open deck and the initial change to the funnel. Note the rangefinder added on the back of the turret and the sighting hoods protected by thick armor.

One of the early changes was the mounting of 76.2mm Lender AA guns atop the main turrets. The elegant lines of the original design provided little space for additional weaponry, a complication that caused the superstructures to become tall and cluttered.

In preparation for transfer to the Black Sea in 1929, **Parizhskaya Kommuna** *received a raised forecastle to improve sea-keeping, but instead it merely scooped up large quantities of water. The structure was removed during a stopover in France, and this photo shows the ship en route to Sevastopol. The lack of freeboard for the casemate guns left them unworkable in heavy seas, a flaw shared by most first-generation dreadnoughts.*

Parizhskaya Kommuna *in Brest. The one foray of a Russian dreadnought into open seas proved dangerous when* Parizhskaya Kommuna *and light cruiser* Profintern *encountered a Force 9 storm in the Bay of Biscay and had to pull into Brest for repairs. The line of portholes indicates the one section of hull that lacked armor plating.*

Parizhskaya Kommuna's *post-transit bow looked graceful in profile, but a front view revealed a less flattering triangular section. Less than successful, it was rebuilt during the ship's 1933 modernization.*

Parizhskaya Kommuna *after her 1930 arrival in the Black Sea. She has a catapult atop her third turret. Notice the gun elevations. It was never standard practice to fire full broadsides.*

Marat *starting to accumulate top-hamper. She was the first of her class to undergo significant modernization. Work lasted from 1928 to 1931 and involved reshaping the forward stack to reduce the smoke problems on the bridge and the addition of the tube-like foremast, which carried a rangefinder station for the modernized fire-control system. The mast proved susceptible to vibrations, and it was not repeated on other ships of the class.*

A modernized Marat *gives a good view of her turret-back rangefinders. Learning their lesson from the failure of* Parizhskaya Kommuna's *light, makeshift bow, the designers gave* Marat *a sturdier structure, which proved more successful.*

Parizhskaya Kommuna, *seen here during the war, has lost the simplicity of her silhouette. Owing to the lack of blast-free deck space, the only way to add new equipment was to build upward.*

Sevastopol *in late form, complete with Lend-Lease radar. Each turret supports three 37mm 70-K anti-aircraft cannon, while large platforms atop the forward and aft conning towers house three 76mm 34-K anti-aircraft guns. The main-battery rangefinder is flanked by secondary rangefinders.*

Parizhskaya Kommuna *hoists one of the ship's boats.*

Left: Oktyabr'skaya Revolyutsiya *under refit at the Baltic factory on 24 June 1933. Her new superstructure has the trunked funnel that forever ruined her silhouette.* Oktyabrina, *as she was nicknamed in the Soviet Fleet, had a conical mast much more resistant to vibration than* Marat's *tube.*

Below: *Close-up of* Parizhskaya Kommuna's *forward superstructure during the Navy Day parade in 1947, showing the auxiliary rangefinders as well as 37mm guns on top of the turrets with the shields removed.*

Oktyabr'skaya Revolyutsiya's *primary contribution to the war effort came as a ground-support artillery platform. Here she is in 1942.*

This late photo shows Parizhskaya Kommuna's *superstructure in full bloom. The main battery rangefinder sits atop the foremast. Gone is the canvas, and the bridge finally has something more substantial to shelter the crew.*

Sevastopol. *The lack of overhang by her casemates shows the extent of the new bulges, which added 2.3m to the ship's beam at the waterline.*

Sevastopol *rides very light, 1944. She has Lend-Lease radars on both masts. Surviving units of the class mounted extensive electronic fits by War's end.*

The remains of the Petropavlovsk *postwar. The bomb hit detonated her forward magazine, killing 326 crewmen, destroying the forward superstructure, and nearly severing the bow. The rest of the ship sank to the bottom; fortunately, she settled less than two meters in the shallow harbor, and the remaining turrets returned to action in less than a month.*

Oktyabr'skaya Revolyutsiya *in wartime form. She mounted perhaps the most powerful AA outfit of any ship in the Soviet fleet: twelve 76mm guns, twenty 37mm cannon, and eight 12.7mm heavy machine guns. The main naval design bureaux, located nearby, took advantage of her as a platform for experimental mounts like the quadruple 37mm 46-K mount on the bow and two twin 76mm 81-K open mounts on the stern – mounts fated never to serve aboard the intended* Sovyetskiy Soyuz *class.*

IZMAIL class

Ship	Builder	Laid Down	Launched	Completed
Izmail	Baltic Works, St. Petersburg	19 Dec 12	22 Jun 15	—
Borodino	Admiralty Works, St. Petersburg	19 Dec 12	31 Jul 15	—
Kinburn	Baltic Works, St. Petersburg	19 Dec 12	30 Oct 15	—
Navarin	Admiralty Works, St. Petersburg	19 Dec 12	9 Nov 16	—

Characteristics: 36,646 tons full, 223.9 x 30.5 x 8.81m, 28.5 knots, 2280nm at 26.5 knots, twelve 356mm/52, twenty-four 130mm/55, four 63mm/35, four 47mm, four 7.62mm mgs, six 450mm torpedo tubes, 1132 men

Given the impossibility of launching a new battleship program, the Bolsheviks searched through their available assets in hopes of a quick fix. A survey of ships wrecked in shallow waters revealed none that warranted further attention. However, several units surviving the War incomplete offered a promising head start. The four *Izmail*-class battlecruisers were far enough along to raise some hopes, and suggestions included a switch to eight 16-inch guns as in the 1915 battleship program. Unfortunately, the lack of resources proved so severe that three of the ships were sold for scrap in 1923. *Izmail* herself survived amid plans for reconstruction as an aircraft carrier, but army-dominated defense policies left her an incomplete hulk until scrapping in the early 1930s.

The *Izmail* design bore a distinct family resemblance to earlier Russian dreadnoughts. The most visible divergence, the raised forecastle, would have decreased wetness forward. Though rated as a battlecruiser (literally, "cruiser of the line"), it had more armor and firepower than *Sevastopol*, albeit on a much greater size. In context with foreign battlecruisers, the protection standards were respectable. Speed lagged behind established norms. However, the 14-inch gun, a proportional upgrade from the 12-inch/52, would have provided firepower beyond that of most contemporary battleships.

The 1930s saw a renewed resolve to build dreadnoughts, and two projects got underway. Project 23 consisted of large but conventional battleships, while Project 69 included two battlecruisers, or "heavy cruisers" in Soviet parlance. Neither project would reach fruition.

Izmail *as she would have appeared – like an enlarged* Sevastopol *but with even less superstructure and twice as many secondary guns.*

Propeller and rudder details on an Izmail*-class ship. Note the auxiliary rudder.*

Kinburn *bow-on before her 1915 launch.*

The newly launched Kinburn *shows the characteristic Russian bow form. None of the* Izmails *progressed far enough to mount any turrets.*

SOVYETSKIY SOYUZ class

Ship	Builder	Laid Down
Sovyetskiy Soyuz	Factory #189 Baltic Works, Leningrad	31 Jul 38
Sovyetskaya Ukraina	Factory #198 Marti South Shipyard, Nikolayev	31 Oct 38
Sovyetskaya Rossiya	Factory #402, Molotovsk	21 Dec 39
Sovyetskaya Byelorussiya	Factory #402, Molotovsk	22 Jul 40

Characteristics: 65,150 tons full, 269.4 x 36.4 x 10.4m, 27.5 knots, 5240nm at 21 knots, nine 406mm/50, twelve 152mm/57, eight 100mm/56, thirty-two 37mm/70, 1664 men

With the major powers restricting themselves by naval treaties, Stalin saw an opportunity to inflate the Soviet Union's stature (and his own) by building ships unfettered by tonnage limitations. However, the artificialities of treaty restraint mattered little compared to the Soviets' genuine inability to build battleships. Difficulties with armor and gun manufacture helped delay the Project 23 ships until the German invasion imposed a more permanent stop. Postwar repair and completion of surviving hulls earned some consideration, but the Soviets had lost faith in their design, and the *Sovyetskiy Soyuz* class went the way of the *Izmail*s by 1949.

Italian influence on the ships showed itself in the slight belt inclination and the cylinders of the Pugliese torpedo protection system. However, the armor scheme showed more concentration than in Italian practice. One odd feature, perhaps intended to eliminate a stern trim, was the gradual thinning of the belt as it extended back along the ship's length.

The Soviets adopted ambitious specifications for the main battery, with heavy shells fired at high velocity. Similar efforts in cruiser-caliber guns gave rise to complications, though a completed *Sovyetskiy Soyuz* might have overcome such hurdles, given enough time. Questions over the quality of materiel and workmanship for these ships make it difficult to gauge their potential value. They might have compensated for their rough edges by virtue of their great size, but in the end, their role remained undefined.

Even before the war, one unit was scrapped incomplete because more than 70,000 hull rivets were found to be defective. Work on the others was delayed by problems in the production of armor, turbines, guns, and even propeller shafts.

Left: *Close-up showing bulkheads for the Italian-designed Pugliese torpedo protection system.*

Below: *Detail of the forward superstructure of the revised Project 23 model with triple-mounted secondaries.*

Right: *Partial construction in the yard. Enthusiasm for Project 23 began evaporating even before War began, canceling any hopes for postwar completions.*

Below: *A worker's-eye vista of a Project 23 ship under construction.*

One of the big guns. The Soviet combination of high velocity and heavy shells would have made for an especially powerful weapon. An 8-inch army howitzer in the lower left corner provides contrast.

KRONSHTADT class

Ship	Builder	Laid Down
Kronshtadt	Factory #194 Marti Shipyard, Leningrad	30 Nov 39
Sevastopol	Factory #200 Marti North Shipyard, Nikolayev	5 Nov 39

Characteristics: 41,539 tons full, 250.5 oa x 31.6 x 8.87m, 32 knots, 8300nm at 14.5 knots, nine 305mm/55, eight 152mm/57, eight 100mm/56, twenty-four 37mm, eight 12.7mm mgs, 1037 men

The Soviets went to extreme lengths to push the *Kronshtadt*-class cruisers through to completion. The original specifications for a ship armed with nine 12-inch/55 guns underwent a thorough recasting to accommodate six German-made 38cm guns, thus increasing firepower while relieving the need for domestically built weaponry. Even so, the project remained problematic as the Soviets struggled to build machinery and armor.

In service aboard the German *Bismarck*-class battleships, the 38cm twin turret proved a practical weapons system. However, it was probably unique – a modern battleship turret so ill armored as to be penetrable by *every* enemy battleship gun at *any* range. For its size, the *Kronshtadt* design suffered from low standards of protection.

The onset of war obviated all such concerns. German invaders captured *Sevastopol* when only about 10% complete. *Kronshtadt's* construction halted during the blockade of Leningrad. The postwar challenge of rehabilitating damaged and incomplete hulls of obsolescent ships did not appeal to the Soviets, who chose instead to break them up.

Project 69-I model as revised to mount German 38cm guns.

Incomplete hull of the "heavy cruiser" Sevastopol *in 1941.*

British *ROYAL SOVEREIGN* class

Ship	Builder	Laid Down	Launched	Completed
Arkhangel'sk (ex-*Royal Sovereign*)	Portsmouth Dockyard	15 Jan 14	29 Apr 15	18 Apr 16

Characteristics: 33,500 tons full, 189 oa x 26.96 x 9.37m, 20.5 knots, 5080nm at 10 knots, eight 381mm/42, eight 152mm/45, eight 102mm/45, twenty-four 40mm/40, forty-six 20mm/70, 1230 men

The Italian surrender in 1943 prompted immediate Soviet claims on Italian naval booty. The Western Allies had numerous reasons – practical, political, and peevish – to delay any deliveries, and the logical alternative was to substitute U.S. and British units available in Britain, units made available because of their marginal value. These served to placate Stalin until an official division of spoils could be worked out in peacetime.

History has not remembered Britain's "R" class battleships with any great respect, through no fault of their own. Following the success of the ambitious and expensive *Queen Elizabeth* class, the "R's" evolved from the older, humbler *Iron Duke* class. The design advances that distinguished the "R's" from *Queen Elizabeth* failed to bring them out from under her shadow, and in fact played a role in casting them as poor cousins in the Royal Navy. The precise reasoning by which the RN chose to let the "R's" fall into neglect remains undocumented, but some factors are apparent.

Royal Sovereign's design deliberately sacrificed stability to gain an easier roll motion, thus improving gunnery. One feature that reduced stability was the new location of the protective deck, mounted one level higher than in previous designs. This had the added benefit of enclosing a larger volume of the hull. Unfortunately, the newly emerging standards of long-range battle meant that this higher deck stood a better chance of being struck and, therefore, penetrated. Typical battleship modernization between the wars would have provided an increased thickness of deck armor to counter such threats, but the increase in topweight would cause a reduction in stability, the exact quality that *Royal Sovereign* had already sacrificed.

With no enthusiasm for these obsolescing ships, the British treated them to minimal upgrades, and by the time of World War II, Churchill was referring to them as "floating coffins." When the time came to provide the Soviets with a battleship, a floating coffin was deemed sufficient.

Though *Royal Sovereign* had not yet sunk into abject decay, steady maintenance could not make a modern ship of her. Perhaps her finest quality lay in her main battery, the 15-inch/42 guns whose reliability and consistent performance earned a place among the great battleship weapons. But here too the lack of modernization hurt her, as her mounts continued with the limited elevation that restricted her ability to engage at longer battle ranges.

She sailed with her new Soviet crew and her new Soviet name on 17 August 1944 for the week-long journey to her new Arctic home. This confirmed her status as a spectator for the remainder of the war. During her year in Soviet war service, *Arkhangel'sk* experienced nothing more exciting than an upgrade to her heating facilities, and she accomplished little except as a distraction to the Germans. From a wartime perspective, she missed her opportunity to harass the German presence along the Norwegian coast, but Stalin had more interest in positioning himself among the postwar naval powers. By 1949, he had received his Italian booty, *Novorossiysk* (ex-*Giulio Cesare*), and sent *Arkhangel'sk* back to Britain.

Arkhangel'sk's 15-inch guns provided the Soviets with an impressive source of firepower, which they had no intention of using.

The British may have enjoyed the irony of lending the Soviets a ship named Royal Sovereign.

Arkhangel'sk *and three old flushdecker destroyers. Britain and America had little enthusiasm for sending the Soviets any modern fleet units.*

CHAPTER 2

Cruisers

The Imperial fleet played an important role in the development of modern cruisers. In the 1870s, the *General Admiral* class pioneered the merchant-raiding armored cruiser – an idea somewhat ahead of its time, as an effective combination of speed and armor lay beyond the grasp of available technologies. Most navies contented themselves with protected cruisers which, relying on deck protection, had no heavy belts to slow them. Nevertheless the Russians continued with a slow but regular succession of armored cruisers, and while the 1890s brought significant advances in propulsion and armor, Russian designs failed to distinguish themselves. The first impressive design was the last – *Ryurik*, designed and built in Britain. Respectable as *Ryurik* was, she entered service the same year as the first of the British battlecruisers, making her obsolescent from the start. Post-Revolution scrapping claimed all the surviving armored cruisers except, ironically, old *Narova* (ex-*General Admiral*).

Strangely, the Russians gave little thought to protected cruisers until the type was in its last years as new steel alloys made belted cruisers the international norm. Still, some of the Imperial navy's finest moments in the Russo-Japanese War derived from the exploits of its protected cruisers which, like the early armored cruisers, provided a threat against merchant shipping.

The light cruiser, which adopted the armored cruiser's belt protection on a more modest scale, took over most of the protected cruiser's roles. Russia came late to the concept and started construction just before World War I. These ships were specialized for fleet scouting and screening rather than high-seas raiding. However, those units that reached completion did so only after protracted delays – from keel-laying to completion, thirteen years at the least – and were consequently out-dated before ever having a chance to perform their mission. Instead they served most importantly as training platforms and testbeds for new equipment.

The first shall be last. Often cited as the first armored cruiser, General Admiral *became* Narova *upon conversion to minelayer in 1909, then* 25 Oktyabrya *in 1922, a time when more recent ships were going to the breakers. Hulked in 1938, she was eventually sunk as a breakwater in the Neva River.*

Resumption of cruiser construction by the Soviets represented a major step in the country's industrial recovery, and the *Kirov* types suffered from the attendant misdirection in technology and administration. Their 180mm guns proved a developmental dead end, and the more conventional 6-inch caliber established itself for wartime and postwar designs.

DIANA class

Ship	Builder	Laid Down	Launched	Completed
Pallada	Galernii Island, St. Petersburg	23 May 97	14 Aug 99	1902
Diana	Galernii Island, St. Petersburg	23 May 97	30 Sep 99	10 Dec 02
Avrora	New Admiralty SY, St. Petersburg	23 May 97	24 May 00	18 Sep 03

Characteristics (1941): 7271 tons full, 126.8 oa x 16.8 x 6.4m, very low speed, nine 130mm/55, two 76.2mm, five 45mm/46, 447 men

Avrora in 1940, 37 years old yet little changed in appearance. Inwardly, however, she was worn out, barely able to move.

The Russians had built only three protected cruisers before a spurt beginning in the 1890s, the time when other navies were embracing belted designs. Fourteen ships entered service by 1907, the *Diana*s being among the first. Their initially weak weaponry prompted a succession of rearmaments. Their lack of speed had no easy remedy.

Pallada became a casualty of the Russo-Japanese War, sunk then salvaged by the Japanese. The other pair survived battles and internment, participated in World War I, and were finally laid up in 1918. *Diana* went to the breakers in 1922, but *Avrora* avoided this fate thanks to a 1917 refit that left her in good condition. Her prominent role in the Revolution made her something of an icon, and she returned to service in 1923 as a training ship with 130mm guns replacing her original 6-inch battery. Decrepitude reduced her to a stationary platform by 1933. She nevertheless persevered through some rough handling during the Great Patriotic War and went on to become a museum ship, extant in Saint Petersburg with her 6-inch guns restored.

Above: *A 1930 view of* Avrora's *aft command post, showing the rangefinder on top and a 76mm Lender anti-aircraft gun. Canvas on the railings provides additional cover.*

Opposite above: *A peaceful scene replayed aboard countless ships over the course of decades.* Avrora's *ammunition rails serve perfectly well as hammock supports. Old-fashioned ventilators and other turn-of-the-century features abound.*

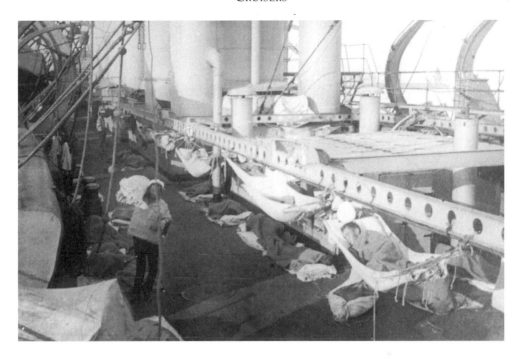

Below: Avrora *looking much sadder in 1942. She has donated her guns to coastal batteries and an armored train. Targeted by German artillery, she suffered multiple hits. Her caretaker crew kept her from capsizing but couldn't prevent her settling to the harbor bottom.*

BOGATYR class

Ship	Builder	Laid Down	Launched	Completed
Bogatyr	Vulcan SY, Stettin	9 Dec 99	17 Jan 01	7 Aug 02
Oleg	New Admiralty SY, St. Petersburg	6 Jul 02	14 Aug 03	12 Oct 04
General Kornilov (ex-*Ochakov*, ex-*Kagul*, ex-*Ochakov*)	Lazarev Admiralty SY, Sevastopol	13 Aug 01	21 Sep 02	10 Jun 09
Komintern (ex-*Kagul*, ex-*Pamiat Merkuriya*)	Admiralty SY, Nikolayev	5 Sep 01	2 Jun 02	Jul 1905
Vityaz	St. Petersburg	1900	—	—

Characteristics (1941): 7838 tons full, 133 oa x 16.61 x 7.2m, 20 (?) knots, 2200nm at 12 knots, eight 130mm/55, three 76.2mm/30, three 45mm/46, two 25mm, five 12.7mm mgs, 195 mines, 490 men

Bogatyr continued the model of the protected cruiser capable of commerce raiding. This was the last class of protected cruisers completed in Russia, and the best – fast and fitted with armor for most of its artillery (eight out of twelve guns). Unfortunately, these twelve guns came in three different mountings – turrets, casemates, and open shields – each with its own rate of fire, making salvo-firing nearly impossible. World War I saw the turrets removed from some ships and a replacement of the original 6-inch battery with sixteen 130mm guns.

By the end of 1920, fate had had its way with the *Bogatyrs*. *Oleg* sat on the bottom of Kronshtadt harbor after damage from British torpedo boats. *Kornilov* had fled to internment in Bizerte with the rest of Wrangel's fleet. *Bogatyr* herself was little more than a hulk, while poor *Vityaz* had never made it to launching, lost in a fire. The only significant ship left behind in the Black Sea was *Pamiat Merkuriya*, immobilized by a conscientious mangling of her machinery by the retreating Allies. Fortunately for her, enough of *Bogatyr* lingered in the Baltic to provide replacement parts. In 1922, the newly renamed *Komintern* returned to service, and the remains of *Bogatyr* went to the breakers.

Komintern served in training through the 1930s and converted for mine laying at the start of the war, by which time she was in a terrible condition. In October 1942 she was scuttled just outside of Poti as a breakwater, though this did not end her career. The following year, the Soviets used her as a platform for a 45mm anti-MTB battery. Sections of the hull remain visible there.

Komintern, *still a viable warship in the 1920s and, as the only Soviet cruiser in the Black Sea, a valuable asset until the more modern* Profintern *transferred there in 1929. Here she carries sixteen 130mm/55 guns, anti-aircraft guns atop her turrets, and a rangefinder above the bridge.*

Boats come alongside in 1935.

Komintern *unloads a torpedo boat. Most large navies considered the idea of using large ships to convey MTBs close to enemy units. For the Soviets, this led ultimately to the never-built* Bloha *design.*

Seen here in her final guise as a minelayer during the war, Komintern *wears elaborate camouflage. Her stacks have been reduced to two, and her 130mm guns to eight. Both turrets have been replaced with single shielded mounts.*

SVETLANA class

Ship	Builder	Laid Down	Launched	Completed
Baltic group				
Krasnyi Krym (ex-Svetlana, ex-Profintern)	Russo-Baltic SB Co., Reval	24 Nov 13	11 Dec 15	1 Jul 28
Pravda (ex-Admiral Butakov)	Putilov SY, St. Petersburg	11 Nov 13	23 Jul 16	—
Admiral Spiridov	Putilov SY, St. Petersburg	16 Nov 13	27 Aug 16	24 Dec 26
Admiral Greig	Russo-Baltic SB Co., Reval	24 Nov 13	26 Nov 16	24 Dec 26
Black Sea group				
Chervona Ukraina (ex-Admiral Nakhimov)	Russud Dockyard, Nikolayev	31 Oct 13	7 Nov 15	21 Mar 27
Krasnyi Kavkaz (ex-Admiral Lazarev)	Russud Dockyard	31 Oct 13	28 Jun 16	21 Jan 32
Admiral Kornilov	Russud Dockyard, Nikolayev	1914	28 Oct 22	—
Admiral Istomin	Russud Dockyard, Nikolayev	1914	—	—

Characteristics (Krasny Krym 1944): 8000 tons full, 158.4 oa x 15.35 x 5.69m, 22 knots, 4400nm at 8 knots, fifteen 130mm/55, six 100mm/50, four 45mm/46, ten 37mm/63, twelve 12.7mm mgs, six 533mm torpedo tubes, 100 mines, 852 men
Characteristics (Krasnyi Kavkaz 1943): 9030 tons full, 169.5 oa x 15.7 x 6.6m, 29 knots, 3000nm at 15 knots, four 180mm/60, twelve 100mm/50, two 76mm/55, four 45mm/46, ten 37mm/63 70K, fourteen 12.7mm mgs, twelve 533mm torpedo tubes, 100 mines, 878 men

Thanks to World War I, the Svetlanas failed to reach completion as a powerful expression of light cruiser design, instead straggling into service as a batch of leftovers. The project began with great potential, introducing turbine machinery to Russia's cruiser force. Lacking the range needed for commerce raiding, these ships would specialize in fleet operations, scouting for the battle line and protecting it from enemy torpedo craft. They could also lay mines, a hallmark of Russian naval warfare. The need to finance the Izmail -class battlecruisers imposed some skimping on the Svetlanas, and their speed requirement fell below 30 knots.

The ships started out to a common design, but the Black Sea units underwent changes while building. Ultimately, the drawn-out business of completing the ships opened the door for conversions unprecedented among fleet units. *Admiral Spiridov* and *Admiral Greig* found themselves diverted entirely from their combatant careers, emerging in 1926 as fast tankers, only vaguely recognizable for their cruiser origins. *Admiral Kornilov* and *Admiral Istomin* had less luck, getting scrapped incomplete in 1927. *Admiral Butakov* was destined for a similar fate, but only after generating rust for forty years. Having been renamed *Pravda* and later *Voroshilov*, her living death finally ended in 1957.

As completed, *Chervona Ukraina* and *Profintern* remained close to the original layout. The urgency to get some cruisers – *any* cruisers – into service forced them to completion to the original design, hardly changed except for their anti-aircraft guns and four triple torpedo launchers. In wartime, they operated more actively than the more valuable modern cruisers, constantly shelling the Germans during the battles for Odessa, Sevastopol, and Feodissiya.

Krasnyi Kavkaz had a different experience. Designers chose her to mount a battery of 180mm guns, weapons of great destructive potential. The provision of only four single turrets limited her capability but at least afforded better prospects than her unmodernised cousins would have against enemy cruisers. The 180mm gun ultimately proved too ambitious. On the other hand, the secondary battery of Italian-designed 100mm guns performed well. Regardless of her limitations, *Krasnyi Kavkaz* gave stellar service, using the full 37km range of her main guns in bombardment duty, shuttling troops around the Black Sea, and even serving as an oversized landing craft, disembarking men straight onto the pier while under fire from German field guns during the assault on Feodossiya.

KIROV class, Project 26 (and see p. 54, Project 26-bis)

Ship	Builder	Laid Down	Launched	Completed
Kirov	#189 Ordzonikidze Factory, Leningrad	22 Oct 35	30 Nov 36	23 Sep 38
Voroshilov	Marti South, Nikolayev	15 Oct 35	28 Jun 37	20 Jun 40

Admiral Greig *under construction at the Russo-Baltic shipyard at Reval. Note the position of the casemates to allow the guns to bow-on fire, a common feature on Russian ships at the time.*

Whither now the cruiser? This is the tanker Grozneft *(ex-Admiral Spiridov) prewar. Without their cruiser belt armor, the high-speed hulls lacked the longitudinal strength for carrying oil, and* Grozneft's *sister-ship* Azneft *(ex-Admiral Greig) broke up in a 1937 storm.*

Looking much like the original design, Profintern *carries her battery of fifteen 130mm/55 guns in Sevastopol in 1932.*

This view shows the fire-control post on the foremast, the canvas-covered bridge common in leftover tsarist ships, and the 100mm Minisini mount on the bow. The Soviets purchased ten of these twin mounts from Italy in 1932 and installed three on each of the Svetlanas.

Close-up of Chervona Ukraina's *superstructure during the late 1930s showing the open rangefinder atop the bridge and a fire-control station and projector platform on the foremast. The least-modified ship of the three,* Chervona Ukraina *had relatively simple fire control.*

Above: *The five years that went into rebuilding* Krasny Kavkaz *gave her a much more modern look. Note the lofty position of her rangefinders, affording an advantage over most light cruisers of the time.*

Left: *Having lost all but one of its Black Sea bases, the Soviet Navy in 1942 had no drydocks there to accommodate a light cruiser.* Krasny Kavkaz *needed repairs after near-miss bombs damaged her stern on 4 January. Workers in Poti improvised, joining two drydocks that together could fit the aft two-thirds of the hull.*

Above: *A Lend-Lease Vickers quad .50-caliber machine gun atop the forward 180mm turret. Note the standard Russian deck planking – short planks held together with metal cross-deck bands.*

Right: *Close-up of a 100mm heavy AA mount aboard* Krasny Kavkaz. *The Soviets adopted the gun mount designed by Italy's prolific engineer Eugenio Minisini based on a gun designed by Skoda for the Austro-Hungarian Navy.*

Krasny Kavkaz in 1943 retains the large cranes despite removal of her catapult and aircraft in a 1939–40 refit. Shadows indicate the two triple torpedo launchers amidships. She carried the heaviest AA weaponry of any ship in the Black Sea: twelve 100mm guns, four 45mm 21-K, fourteen 37mm 70-K, two quad Vickers, and six single DShK 0.50-caliber machine guns.

MAXIM GORKIY class, Project 26-bis

Ship	Builder	Laid Down	Launched	Completed
Maxim Gorkiy	Ordzonikidze, Leningrad	20 Dec 36	30 Apr 38	25 Oct 40
Molotov	Marti South, Nikolayev	14 Jan 37	19 May 39	14 Jun 41
Kalinin	Amur, Komsomolsk	12 Jun 38	8 May 42	31 Dec 42
Kaganovich	Amur, Komsomolsk	26 Aug 38	7 May 44	6 Dec 44

Characteristics (Kirov 1944): 9440 tons full, 191.3 oa x 17.66 x 6.15m, 35.94 knots, 3750nm at 17.8 knots, nine 180mm/57, eight 100mm/56, ten 37mm/63 70-K, fourteen 12.7mm mgs, six 533mm torpedo tubes, 164 mines, 872 men
Characteristics (Molotov 1944): 9780 tons full, 191.4 oa x 17.54 x 7.2m, 36.3 knots max, 3859nm at 16.8 knots, nine 180mm/57, six 100mm/56, six 45mm/46, twelve 37mm/63, twelve 12.7mm mgs, six 533mm torpedo tubes, 164 mines, 862 men

Construction of a cruiser represented a milestone in Soviet industrial recovery. The project got underway with confidence based on experience bringing *Krasnyi Kavkaz* into service. However, the new ships would inherit little from this background apart from the 180mm caliber guns. In fact, the *Kirov*s owed more to the Italians than to any domestic forebear, and the project treated the Italians to a close-up look at Soviet decision-making. Project 26 may have set the record for administrative fumbling.

Having acquired a fondness for Italy's cruisers, the Soviets negotiated an agreement for drawings and components of the *Raimondo Montecuccoli* class – which promised a timely delivery of defect-free turbines for the first ship, a phenomenon previously unknown in the Red navy – while design and construction would take place in Russia with assistance from Italian technicians.

Friction between buyer and seller was immediate and ongoing. The Soviets suddenly announced they wanted, not *Montecuccoli*'s engines, but those of the next Italian cruiser class, *Eugenio di Savoia*. When disagreement over some of the design documentation could not be settled by diplomacy, bribery sufficed instead. The Russians refused to accept the Italian system of hull framing. (And rightly so. Less attentive adaptation of Italian hull design for the Project 7 destroyers would produce severe consequences.) The switch from *Montecuccoli*'s armament of four 152mm twin mounts became something of an epic.

The naval treaty system that developed between the World Wars imposed strict definitions on cruisers, with limits on ships authorized to carry 155mm and 203mm guns. Having been excluded from these treaty conferences, the Soviets saw an opportunity in mounting 180mm guns aboard their light cruisers, which were limited to 155mm guns in the treaty navies. Project 26 began with its armament concentrated into three twin mounts – only six guns to *Montecuccoli*'s eight, but with a broadside advantage of 585kg to 400kg.

Then came the decision that six guns weren't enough; the turrets would house three guns each, with minimal alteration to other features. Commendable design work created a triple turret only 30 tons heavier than the twin, and the leadership got what it wanted, a nine-gun *Kirov*. It also got cramped gun mounts with poor rates of fire and increased dispersal from the closely spaced guns.

As a prestige project, *Kirov* enjoyed unrivaled preference in the supply of top-quality components, with a consequently quick construction time. Her sister-ships, less privileged, still proceeded to completion as quickly as the industry would allow. Schedules for the two Far East units suffered owing to the immature construction base there and the German invasion.

The Project 26-bis featured a redesigned superstructure, thickened belt and turret armor (70mm vs. 50mm), and improved fire control. On paper, the *Kirov*s seem a reasonable match for like-sized foreign types, but the war never provided a showcase for their sea-battle brawn, casting them instead as gunfire-support platforms, fast transports, and anti-aircraft guardships.

Voroshilov *in wartime. The main-battery rangefinder tops the foremast, with stabilized anti-aircraft directors below on each side. British Lend-Lease radars bristle atop her masts and rangefinders: a Type 281 aircraft-warning radar, a Type 284 and two Type 285 surface gunnery radars, and two Type 282 AA gunnery radars.*

A bomb struck Kirov *on 24 April 1942, damaging the mainmast, the after stack, and every one of the 100mm mounts in her crowded secondary battery.*

A political meeting beneath the guns of Kirov's *aft turret. She wears a covering of tarps to camouflage her from German eyes. Note the temporary replacement mainmast.*

Kalinin *during the short period of fighting against Japan. Wartime supply problems were especially pronounced in construction of the two Pacific cruisers; propeller shafts had to be unearthed from the rubble of a Stalingrad factory. The lack of the 100mm guns left the cruisers mounting eight 85mm 92-K guns instead.*

A KOR-2 flying boat on Molotov's *catapult in 1941. The cruisers rarely used their aircraft, in some cases trading them for additional anti-aircraft weapons.*

Voroshilov *no longer has a catapult in 1942, but she has more AA weaponry. By 1943, she mounted three 45mm/46 21-K and sixteen 37mm/63 70-K guns, as well as six DShK and two quad Vickers 12.7mm machine guns. Note the concentration of the 100mm mounts.*

On the second day of the war, Maxim Gorkiy *lost her bows on a mine in the Irben Straits. She withdrew under her own power while subjected to German air attack. A section of Project 68 bow was grafted on, and repairs took only 43 days. The Soviets demanded higher standards than the Italians for their cruiser hull framing, and all the* Kirovs *survived the war.*

CHAPAYEV class, Project 68

Ship	Builder	Laid Down	Launched	Completed
Chapayev	Factory #189 Bal'tiyske Ob'yedineniye, Leningrad	8 Oct 39	28 Apr 41	16 May 50
Valery Chkalov (ex-*Chkalov*)	Factory #189 Bal'tiyske Ob'yedineniye, Leningrad	31 Aug 39	25 Oct 47	5 Nov 50
Zheleznyakov	Factory #194 Marti, Leningrad	31 Oct 39	25 Jul 41	19 Apr 50
Frunze	Factory #198 (#444) Marti, Nikolayev	29 Aug 39	30 Dec 40	19 Dec 50
Kuybyshev	Factory #200 61 Kommunar, Nikolayev	31 Aug 39	31 Jan 41	20 Apr 50
Ordzhonikidze	Factory #198 (#444) Marti, Nikolayev	31 Dec 40	—	—
Sverdlov	Factory #200 61 Kommunar, Nikolayev	31 Dec 40	—	—
Zhdanov	Factory #189 Bal'tiyske Ob'yedineniye, Leningrad	—	—	—

Lenin	Factory #189 Bal'tiyske Ob'yedineniye, Leningrad	—	—	—
Dzerzhinski	Factory #189 Bal'tiyske Ob'yedineniye, Leningrad	—	—	—
Lazo	#199 Amurski Shipyard, Komsomol'sk-na-Amure	—	—	—
Avrora	Factory #194 Marti, Leningrad	—	—	—
Parkhomenko	Factory #200 61 Kommunar, Nikolayev	—	—	—
Shchors	#199 Amurski Shipyard, Komsomol'sk-na-Amure	—	—	—
Shcherbakov	Factory #198 (#444) Marti, Nikolayev.	—	—	—
Kotovski	Factory #200 61 Kommunar, Nikolayev	—	—	—

Characteristics (as designed): 13,420 tons full, 199 oa x 18.7 x 6.5m, 33.2 knots, 4400 at 17 knots, twelve 152mm/57, eight 100mm/56, twelve 37mm/63, eight 12.7mm mgs, six 533mm torpedo tubes, 742 men

Project 68 began with the high hopes that characterized Soviet naval plans in the 1930s, with a total of twenty-six ships planned. Then reality stepped in – only seven keels laid and four hulls launched before the start of the war. The exact number of orders remains uncertain, as do the identities of the builders. *Kuybyshev*'s construction involved as many as three yards.

The 180mm gun had become a complication as the Soviets tried to enter the interwar system of naval treaties, tailored to the international convention of 6-inch and 8-inch armaments. This diplomatic issue and the gun's technical problems made the switch to 152mm a logical one. Unfortunately, as was often the case, technical issues lagged behind the official pronouncements: the 152mm gun existed only on paper. Optimism inspired a proposal to Germany for the purchase of 150mm triple turrets to outfit two ships (redesignated Project 68I), but the optimism and the proposal fizzled before the end of the 1940. Ironically, the wartime construction delays gave gun designers time to catch up.

Chapayev developed from the *Kirov* lineage, and designers made good use of that experience along with the harsher lessons of battle. Ships waited five years after War's end for completion to the modified Project 68K standard, but the final product proved worth the wait. Project 68K showed a common-sensical blend of firepower, protection, and mobility.

Family resemblance between Kirovs *and* Chapayevs *was strong enough to allow transplants on two occasions. Here is* Frunze *drydocked in 1943, in the process of sacrificing her stern for repair of the damaged* Molotov.

The Project 68K modification improved Zheleznyakov's *fire control, electronics, and anti-aircraft weapons. The* Chapayevs' *sea-keeping qualities helped make them popular ships.*

German *HIPPER* class, Project 83

Ship	Builder	Laid Down	Launched	Completed
Tallin (ex-*Lützow*)	Deschimag, Bremen	2 Aug 37	1 Jul 39	—

Characteristics (as designed, except artillery as of 1941): 18,400 tons full, 212.2 x 21.7 x 7.2m, 32.5 knots, 5050nm at 15 knots, four 203mm/60, two 37mm, eight 20mm Oerlikons, 1600 men

In February 1940, the strange and deadly relationship between Germany and the Soviet Union fathered an agreement by which the Germans would receive roughly 3.5 million tons of food and raw materials in exchange for warship plans, gun turrets, and various other drawings, materiel, and gizmos. The Germans began falling behind in their deliveries almost immediately, but in April the cruiser ex-*Lützow*, the largest item on the list, successfully reached Leningrad at the end of a towline. The Soviets had known Cruiser "L" would arrive incomplete, but they had negotiated for her to come with all her main battery. In fact, she mounted just two turrets, only one of which had its guns in place.

Naming the ship *Petropavlovsk* in September, the Soviets hoped to complete her by mid-1942, but the Germans overturned this plan with a different sort of delivery, Operation Barbarossa of June 1941. Equipped by then with a second pair of guns, *Petropavlovsk* supported the defense of Leningrad by bombarding the approaching enemy, which resulted in counter-fire that landed multiple hits and caused the ship to sink to the harbor bottom. Salvage work eventually returned her to action, and her name switched to *Tallin* in September 1944.

The largest heavy cruisers to see action in World War II, the *Hipper*s had more size than actual capability. Their 8-inch guns and fire-control system performed well, and the main battery armor had respectable thickness, but the hull had little protection. *Prinz Eugen*, *Lützow*'s sister-ship, suffered propulsion unreliability of legendary proportions, but the Soviet ship had different machinery and might have escaped the worst problems. This remains a subject for speculation as *Tallin* never became fully operational. Though the Soviets in 1945 captured *Seydlitz*, a sister-ship which the Germans had begun converting to an aircraft carrier, little postwar thought went to completing a version of either ship.

Though never fully operational, she went through four names in Soviet service: Petropavlovsk, Tallin, Dnepr, *and* PKZ 112.

Prinz Eugen *shows what a completed* Tallin *would look like. Her gunnery at the Battle of Denmark Strait proved the potential of the design's weaponry. – courtesy of WGAZ Marineschule Mürwik.*

American *OMAHA* class

Ship	Builder	Laid Down	Launched	Completed
Murmansk (ex-*Milwaukee*)	Todd Shipyards, Seattle	13 Dec 18	24 Mar 21	20 Jun 23

Characteristics: 10,460 tons full, 169.4 x 16.86 x 4.11m, 30 knots, 7080nm at 15 knots, ten 152mm/53, six 76mm/50, six 40mm/56, twelve 20mm Oerlikon, six 533 torpedo tubes, 805 men.

As a surrogate pending the allocation of an Italian cruiser, *Milwaukee* joined the Northern Fleet on 20 April 1944. Unlike *Royal Sovereign*, whose great potential as a battleship had fallen into obsolescence, *Murmansk* rated as a flop from the start.

Following a decade-long vacation from cruiser construction, American planners scrambled to put together a set of requirements for a fleet scout. Given the lack of recent precedents, almost any suggestion earned consideration – armor or no armor, numerous small guns or two 14-inch guns, and so on. In the end, the cruiser project fractured into two unfortunate classes, the *Omaha*s and the *Lexington*s, both among the worst American warship designs of the century.

As scouts, the *Omaha*s at least showed commendable mobility – good seaboats, though wet, with admirable speed and range. The late appearance of a twin turret did not spare the design from a set of obsolescent casemate mounts configured to maximize end-on fire. The enclosed positions gave an advantage at a time when open shields were the norm, but neither the mounts nor the magazines had any armor. Only the propulsion spaces and the steering compartment had noteworthy protection, steel-laminate boxes that could defeat most splinters and destroyer-caliber shells, but little else. The few *Omaha*s subjected to battle damage early in the Pacific War quickly established that they had no business venturing into harm's way.

The Soviets did not show the same protectiveness and affection toward *Murmansk* that they lavished on *Arkhangel'sk*. Still, the cruiser's value lay more in her modern equipment than in her old hull. She returned to American custody in 1949, replaced in Soviet service by the ex-Italian cruiser *Emanuele Filiberto Duca d'Aosta*.

Murmansk *during the war. Despite the antique appearance, she carried considerable anti-aircraft armament.*

The Soviets examined Murmansk's *extensive electronics in great detail. – courtesy of Arseny Malov.*

CHAPTER 3

Destroyers

The Russians made history's first successful attack with a locomotive torpedo during the fight with Turkish forces in 1878 and, given the ongoing need to counter threats from the premier fleets in the 19th century, built a hoard of torpedo boats. These small vessels enjoyed a short period of popularity but limited real-world value. Larger designs followed, and during the Russo-Japanese War, construction began on a batch of eighteen hefty destroyers, four related classes competitive with the newest foreign types. Though these ships fell behind the rapid development in destroyer design during World War I, surviving units continued in secondary duties into the 1950s.

NOVIK classes

Ship	Builder	Laid Down	Launched	Completed
Yakov Sverdlov (ex-*Novik*)	Putilov SY, St. Petersburg	1 Aug 10	4 Jul 11	4 Oct 13
Schastlivyi class				
Frunze (ex-*Bystry*)	Vaddon Factory, Kherson	29 Oct 13	7 Jun 14	1 May 15
Izyaslav class				
Karl Marx (ex-*Izyaslav*, ex-*Gromonosets*)	Böcker, Revel	19 Sep 13	22 Nov 14	29 Jun 17
Kalinin (ex-*Pryamyslav*)	Böcker, Revel	19 Sep 13	9 Aug 15	20 Jul 27

Gavriil class				
Voikov (ex-*Leitnenant Il'in*, ex-*Garibaldi*, ex-*Trotski*)	Putilov SY, St. Petersburg	1 Jul 13	28 Nov 14	13 Dec 16
Karl Libknekht (ex-*Kapitan Belli*)	Putilov SY, St. Petersburg	28 Jul 13	23 Oct 15	3 Aug 28
Valeryan Kuibyshev (ex-*Kapitan Kern*, ex-*Rykov*)	Putilov SY, St. Petersburg	4 Dec 13	27 Aug 15	15 Oct 27
Lenin (ex-*Kapitan Izylmetev*)	Putilov SY, St. Petersburg	1 Dec 13	3 Nov 14	23 Jul 16
Orfei class				
Artiom (ex-*Azard*, ex-*Zinoviev*)	Metal Works, St. Petersburg	Jul 1915	5 Jun 16	23 Oct 16
Engels (ex-*Desna*)	Metal Works, St. Petersburg	Nov 1914	7 Nov 15	29 Aug 16
Stalin (ex-*Samson*)	Metal Works, St. Petersburg	13 Jul 15	5 Jun 16	4 Dec 16
Uritskii (ex-*Zabiyaka*)	Metal Works, St. Petersburg	Nov 1913	5 Nov 14	27 Nov 15
Volodarskii (ex-*Pobeditel*)	Metal Works, St. Petersburg	Nov 1913	5 Nov 14	7 Nov 15
Kerch class				
Dzerzhinskiy (ex-*Kaliakriya*)	Russud SY, Nikolayev	11 Nov 15	23 Aug 16	12 Nov 17
Nezamozhnik (ex-*Zante*, ex-*Nezamozhnyi*)	Russud SY, Nikolayev	May 1916	3 Apr 17	7 Nov 23
Shaumyan (ex-*Levkas*)	Russud SY, Nikolayev	5 Jun 16	23 Oct 17	10 Dec 25
Zheleznyakov (ex-*Korfu*, ex-*Petrovskii*)	Russud SY, Nikolayev	5 Jun 16	23 Oct 17	10 Jun 25

Characteristics (Yakov Sverdlov 1940): 1597 tons normal, 102.43 oa x 9.53 x 3.45m, 30.48 knots, 1800nm at 16 knots, four 102mm/60, one 76mm/30 8-K, four 45mm/46, four 12.7mm mgs, nine 450mm torpedo tubes, 50 mines, 168 men

The Ukraina *class of 1904 represented Russia's first effort at large destroyer design. Three units survived after 1922, and all fell prey to ideological renaming.* Vojskovoi *became* Fridrich Engels, *then* Vojskovoi *again, and finally* Markin*. She finished her career as a Caspian gunboat, her original armament replaced by a trio of 102mm guns aft.*

Sladkov *(ex-*Vsadnik*) of the* Gaidamak *class. Like the other seventeen destroyers in her program,* Sladkov *traded her original 11-pounders for powerful 102mm/60 guns just prior to World War I. She served as a gunboat during the civil war and was scrapped in 1926.*

Of all the pre-Novik destroyers, the Okhotnik-*class* Konstruktor *(ex-Sibirskii Stryelok) experienced the most dramatic alteration, thanks to German bombers that removed her bow in November 1941. Hastily repaired and 12m shorter, she resumed her duties as an escort vessel.*

Frunze *had the typical features of later Black Sea Noviks: the canvas-enclosed bridge, a torpedo armament of nine tubes, and four 102mm guns – one forward and three aft, including the superfiring mount.*

Twice the tonnage of Russia's previous destroyers, *Novik* entered service with weaponry and speed unprecedented in any navy. Some inspiration may have come from Britain's *Swift* of 1907, which boasted four 4-inch guns and a speed of 35 knots, managing these feats by displacing 2170 tons; even so, she turned out an impractical "one-off." In contrast, *Novik*'s ambitious design suffered only minor problems – overweight increased her draft by about eight inches and helped make her a wet seaboat – and she became the prototype for a series of orders totaling sixty-five additional units, of which thirty-six eventually reached completion. (The table above reflects only those units in service after 1920.) *Frunze* and *Dzerzhinskiy* had sunk during the Revolution, being salvaged and returned to service in 1927 and 1929 respectively.

Novik's follow-ons had three funnels rather than her four, and their hull contours made them drier. Units intended for Black Sea duty emphasized torpedoes, originally boasting five twin torpedo launchers; equipped with only three guns, they had partial compensation in being the only *Novik*s with a superfiring mount.

Not all changes were improvements. None of the *Schastlivyi*s reached their designed speed, and the Böcker ships saved money by reducing bulkheads. Structural strength sometimes took a back seat to demands for increased

In 1940, Lenin retired from the active squadrons, reclassified as a training destroyer. Under repair at Libau in June 1941 and unable to evacuate, she was scuttled.

Stalin *wears identification letters on her hull, a practice that ended with the start of the war. The three guns crowding on the quarterdeck mark her as a Baltic unit.*

A closer look at Stalin's *guns. The 102mm mounts were modified after World War I to increase elevation.*

Above and right: *The Soviets never bowed to technological orthodoxy. They sketched a 15-ton flying submarine; they considered torpedoes carrying a payload of carrier pigeons; and they tested a 305mm recoilless rifle aboard the destroyer* Engels *in 1934.*

The Black Sea destroyer Dzerzhinski *at full speed, making plenty of smoke as her crew mans the rails. The photo shows the ship in the 1930s before the wartime addition of antiaircraft weaponry.*

Dzerzhinski *in 1941 alongside a Project 7 destroyer.*

weaponry. While building, *Izyaslav* had her intended complement of two guns and twelve torpedo tubes increased by three tubes shortly before her launch date, then switched to three guns and twelve tubes the next summer a few days before it became four guns and nine tubes. She gained an extra gun soon after commissioning.

The ships excelled in firepower. The international norm for destroyer weaponry had begun its increase from 3-inch to 4-inch, and *Novik* trumped all others by adopting a 60-caliber model whose high velocity maximized accuracy and striking energy. Nine tubes represented a powerful torpedo armament (*Swift* carried only two tubes) and, with the addition of minelaying gear, turned the *Novik*s into the ideal tool for Baltic warfare.

Novik had additional significance as the first Russian destroyer with turbine engines and oil-fired boilers. Such advances, in company with other impressive designs like the *Izmail*s and *Svetlana*s, showed that the Russian fleet had potential to become a powerful and balanced force.

LENINGRAD class: Project 1

Ship	Builder	Laid Down	Launched	Completed
Leningrad	#190 Zhdanov Yard, Leningrad	5 Nov 32	17 Nov 33	5 Dec 36
Moskva	#198 Marti Factory, Nikolayev	29 Oct 32	30 Oct 34	10 Aug 38
Kharkov	#198 Marti Factory, Nikolayev	29 Oct 32	9 Sep 34	19 Nov 38
Minsk class, Project 38				
Minsk	#190 Zhdanov Yard, Leningrad	5 Oct 34	6 Nov 35	15 Feb 39
Project 38bis				
Tblisi (ex-*Tiflis*)	#198 Marti Factory, Nikolayev	15 Jan 35	24 Jul 39	11 Dec 40
Baku (ex-*Kiev*, ex-*Ordzhonikidze*, ex-*Sergo Ordzhonikidze*)	#198 Marti Factory, Nikolayev	15 Jan 35	27 Jul 38	27 Dec 39

Characteristics: 2282 tons normal, 122.2 wl x 11.7 x 4.18m, 43 knots, 2100 nm at 20 knots, five 130mm/50, two 76.2mm/55, four 37mm/70, two 12.7mm mgs, eight 533mm torpedo tubes, 84 mines, 344 men

The first project of the new, centralized Special Design Office included some respectable features like longitudinal hull framing and a unit machinery arrangement. Meticulous calculations resulted in a design completed at the proper weight – a Soviet rarity. The ships actually exceeded their ambitious 40-knot speed requirement. Their success is remarkable given the uniquely Soviet hurdles they had to overcome.

Construction times were absurdly long, due partly to mismanagement. The gun design process began in the year after *Leningrad* was laid down, and production of the turbines got rolling only after she'd been launched. Defective components caused further delays, some items reaching a 90% rejection rate, and the problems snowballed as materiel sat waiting for installation and degrading all the while.

At the end of this drama, the Soviets had a set of large flotilla leaders, 10 knots faster than the *Novik*s they were nominally intended to lead. On the negative side, they proved susceptible to shock damage due to inadequate boiler foundations. They lacked sea-keeping. A vulnerability to air attack led to removal of one 130mm gun to accommodate AA additions in some ships. Minor revisions worked into the design after the initial Project 1 trio, but the *Leningrad*s probably mattered more as industrial stepping-stones than for their combat value.

Opposite above: Leningrad *postwar, showing her wartime additions of AA weaponry. She has a twin 76mm 81-K anti-aircraft gun from damaged battleship* Marat *installed on her stern as well as 37mm 70-K AA guns with gunshields mounted all over the superstructure. The characteristic stern facilitated minelaying. – courtesy of Arseny Malov.*

Baku *in 1943.* Baku *took part in a unique voyage when she transferred with two Project 7 destroyers from the Pacific to the Northern Fleet through the heavy ice of the Arctic route.*

Kharkov *during World War II. The* Leningrads *were the first Soviet destroyers to mount the new 130mm/50 gun, a major factor in delaying their completion –* Leningrad *was launched in 1933, and the gun was accepted into the service in 1936. The 50-caliber model attempted to pack the performance of the earlier 130mm/55 gun into a shorter barrel, with a host of resultant problems. A lengthy campaign of correction set things in order before the war broke out.*

Crews man the 37mm cannon and a Lend-Lease water-cooled Browning 0.50-caliber machine gun in the foreground – a drill situation rather than combat, as indicated by the cooks chatting on deck near the torpedo triple mount.

Leningrad at full speed shortly after completion showing her designation code, her square gunshields, and an absence of AA guns.

GNEVNYI class, Project 7

Ship	Builder	Laid Down	Launched	Completed
Gnevnyi	#190 Zhdanov Yard, Leningrad	8 Dec 35	13 Jul 36	23 Dec 38
Groznyi	#190 Zhdanov Yard, Leningrad	21 Dec 35	31 Jul 36	9 Dec 38
Gromkiy	#190 Zhdanov Yard, Leningrad	29 Apr 36	6 Dec 37	31 Dec 38
Gordyi	#190 Zhdanov Yard, Leningrad	25 Jun 36	10 Jun 37	23 Dec 38
Gremyashchiy	#190 Zhdanov Yard, Leningrad	23 Jul 36	12 Aug 37	28 Aug 38
Steregushchiy	#190 Zhdanov Yard, Leningrad	12 Aug 36	18 Jan 38	30 Oct 39
Grozyashchiy	#190 Zhdanov Yard, Leningrad	18 Jun 36	5 Jan 37	17 Sep 39
Stremitelnyi	#189 Ordzhonikidze Yard, Leningrad	22 Aug 36	4 Feb 37	18 Nov 38

Sokrushitelnyi	#189 Ordzhonikidze Yard, Leningrad	29 Oct 36	23 Aug 37	13 Aug 39
Smetlivyi	#189 Ordzhonikidze Yard, Leningrad	17 Sep 36	16 Jul 37	6 Nov 38
Lovkii	#189 Ordzhonikidze Yard, Leningrad	17 Sep 36	—	—
Legkiy	#189 Ordzhonikidze Yard, Leningrad	16 Oct 36	—	—
Bodryi	#198 Marti Factory, Nikolayev	31 Dec 35	1 Aug 36	6 Nov 38
Bystryi	#198 Marti Factory, Nikolayev	17 Apr 36	5 Nov 36	7 Mar 39
Boikiy	#198 Marti Factory, Nikolayev	17 Apr 36	29 Oct 36	9 Mar 39
Besposhchadnyi	#198 Marti Factory, Nikolayev	15 May 36	5 Dec 36	2 Oct 39
Bezuprechnyi	#200 61 Kommunar, Nikolayev	23 Aug 36	25 Jun 37	2 Oct 39
Bditel'nyi	#200 61 Kommunar, Nikolayev	23 Aug 36	29 Jun 37	22 Oct 39
Burnyi	#200 61 Kommunar, Nikolayev	17 Aug 36	—	—
Boevoy	#200 61 Kommunar, Nikolayev	17 Aug 36	—	—
Pronzitel'nyi	#200 61 Kommunar, Nikolayev	15 Oct 36	—	—
Porazhayuschii	#200 61 Kommunar, Nikolayev	25 Dec 36	—	—
Rezvyi	#198 Marti Factory, Nikolayev	5 Nov 35	24 Sep 37	24 Jan 40
Reshitelnyi (i)	#198 Marti Factory, Nikolayev	5 Nov 35	18 Oct 37	—
Rastropnyi	#198 Marti Factory, Nikolayev	27 Feb 36	25 Jun 38	5 Jan 40
Raziashchii	#198 Marti Factory, Nikolayev	27 Feb 36	24 Mar 38	20 Dec 40
R'yaniy	#198 Marti Factory, Nikolayev	31 Dec 35	31 May 37	11 Aug 39

Rezkiy	#198 Marti Factory, Nikolayev	5 May 36	29 Apr 40	16 Aug 42
Retivyi	#198 Marti Factory, Nikolayev	23 Aug 36	27 Sep 39	10 Oct 41
Reshitelnyi (ii) (ex-Pospeshnyi)	#198 Marti Factory, Nikolayev	23 Aug 36	30 Apr 40	5 Sep 41
Revnostnyi (ex-Provornyi)	#198 Marti Factory, Nikolayev	23 Aug 36	22 May 41	14 Dec 41
Raz'yaryonnyi (ex-Peredovoi, ex-Razvitoy)	#198 Marti Factory, Nikolayev	15 Sep 36	22 May 41	14 Dec 41
Rekordnyi (ex-Prytkii)	#198 Marti Factory, Nikolayev	25 Sep 36	6 Apr 39	9 Jan 41
Redkiy (ex-Pylkii)	#198 Marti Factory, Nikolayev	28 Sep 36	28 Sep 41	29 Nov 42
Razumnyi (ex-Prochnyi)	#200 61 Kommunar, Nikolayev	7 Jul 36	30 Jun 39	7 Nov 41

Characteristics: 2215 tons full, 112.8 oa x 10.2 x 4.8m, 38.6 knots, 2640nm at 19 knots, four 130mm/50, two 76mm/55, two 45mm/46, two 12.7 mm mgs, six 533mm torpedo tubes, 65 mines, 236 men

The most numerous class of large warships built in the Soviet Union in the 1930s would have included even more ships if not for industrial limitations and administrative meddling at the highest levels. Project 7 began with a resolve to avoid some of the blind alleys followed in the design of the *Leningrad*s. Officials approached the Italian firms of Ansaldo and Odero and came back with the plans for the Italian destroyer *Maestrale*. From this they borrowed the machinery layout and the overall look of the ship; everything else, for better or for worse, was designed in the Soviet Union.

Despite the difficulties in providing equipment for the handful of *Leningrad*s, plans called for fifty-three Project 7 ships for completion by 1938 – a fine indicator of the gulf between the leadership's comprehension and the actual capabilities of Soviet industry. The excess ambition took its toll on the twenty-eight ships that *were* built. Turbine manufacture, always demanding work, became an ongoing problem. Worse was the weight issue. The original specification called for a standard displacement of 1425 tons; as detail design progressed, it was found that the tonnage had inflated 10%. This could not help the ships' sea-keeping or the structural issue – the careful adaptation of the cruiser *Kirov*'s framing to Russian standards was not pursued with the same zeal in the *Gnevnyi*s. *Gromkiy* survived having her bow nearly ripped off by stormy seas; *Sokrushitelnyi* did not survive when her stern parted between the two aft guns. This hull weakness, however, did not mean the ships crumpled at the first instance of battle damage. From twenty incidents of mine or torpedo damage, only nine losses resulted, and two ships managed to survive lost ends.

The Project 7s were acknowledged sea-keeping inferiors of the *Noviks*, better seaboats with stronger hulls and more stability. But the *Gnevnyi*s had the advantage of their more powerful weaponry, modern fire control, and greater range. Ultimately, given the realities of the Great Patriotic War, there was little advantage for the newer, bigger design.

Twelve ships intended for Pacific duty were prefabricated at Marti Nikolayev and shipped east for final assembly. This proved unfortunate for *Reshitelnyi* (i), still awaiting finishing touches when thrown onto the rocks while under tow in 1938.

The Northern Fleet's Gremyashchiy *in 1942 shows off her striking camo scheme while laying a smoke screen at high speed. One of the earlier ships of the class, she carries square gunshields. She hasn't yet received her AA augmentations.*

The remains of Bditel'ny *in Novorossiysk after the air raid that also claimed* Tashkent. *The forward 130mm guns have already been salvaged. Bombs hit* Bditel'ny *amidships; she suffered an explosion in her aft magazines and the detonation of two torpedoes in the forward launcher, breaking her back.*

A column of Baltic Project 7 destroyers in 1941. Note the rangefinder in the foreground and the 76mm 34-K heavy AA gun abaft the funnel.

A 37mm 70-K anti-aircraft gun aboard Boykii. *This gun, derived from the 25mm Bofors purchased in Sweden in the mid-1930s, entered production only in 1940–41, so the Soviet Navy went to war with its semi-automatic 45mm 21-K gun firing a contact-fuzed shell.*

Veteran Grozyashchii *in 1944 with a third 76mm 34-K gun added on her stern and several 37mm 70-K guns on the superstructure to increase her anti-aircraft defenses. She's recovered from wounds, as the shield for the aft 130mm gun has been replaced or repaired with a rounded type.*

Sokrushitelny *underway in the Baltic showing yet another camouflage scheme. With no class-standardized camouflage, Soviet ships displayed much individual variation.*

Razyaryenny *in 1942 mounting the 130mm guns that formed the Project 7 main battery. Trial-and-error efforts to improve barrel life of the 50-caliber model (initially just 130 rounds) eventually settled on the simple solution of deepening the grooves in the liner. The gun became a good performer, serving in destroyers and coast defense emplacements into the 1980s.*

TASHKENT class, Project 20

Ship	Builder	Laid Down	Launched	Completed
Tashkent	OTO, Livorno	11 Jan 37	28 Dec 37	22 Oct 39

KIEV class, Project 48

Ship	Builder	Laid Down	Launched	Completed
Kiev	#198 Marti Factory, Nikolayev	29 Sep 39	Dec 1940	—
Erevan	#198 Marti Factory, Nikolayev	Dec 1939	Jun 1941	—
Stalinabad	#190 Zhdanov Yard, Leningrad	27 Dec 39	—	—
Petrozavodsk	#198 Marti Factory, Nikolayev	—	—	—
Ochakov	#198 Marti Factory, Nikolayev	—	—	—
Perekop	#198 Marti Factory, Nikolayev	—	—	—
Ashkhabad	#190 Zhdanov Yard, Leningrad	—	—	—
Alma-Ata	#190 Zhdanov Yard, Leningrad	—	—	—
Arkhangel'sk	#402 Factory, Molotovsk	—	—	—
Murmansk	#402 Factory, Molotovsk	—	—	—

Characteristics: 4175 tons full, 133.3 pp x 13.7 x 4m, 43.53 knots, 5030nm at 20 knots, six 130mm/50, two 76.2mm/55, six 37mm/67, six 12.7mm mg, nine 533mm torpedo tubes, 110 mines, 250 men

The Italian navy, aware of France's *Fantasque* and *Mogador* super-destroyer classes, decided in 1935 to build a "scout" class of 2800 tons developed from the *Maestrale*-class destroyers. But when emphasis shifted to planning a fleet for operations beyond the Mediterranean, this scout was superseded by the larger "Capitani Romani" class. Rather than simply throw out the scout design, the Italians put it on the export market. The Soviets found it promising and, after two years of contract wrangling, placed an order for one ship from OTO, to be followed by Italian assistance in starting construction in domestic yards. A plan for three *Tashkent* replicas was dropped in favor of the Project 48, which adapted the design to Soviet practice.

Having personally witnessed the pre-trials greasing of cruiser *Montecuccoli*'s hull, the Soviets understood the exaggeration in Italian speed claims. *Tashkent* had a 42.5-knot specification, and she hit 43.5 knots while running trials without her guns installed. She arrived in the Black Sea at the end of 1939 still without her main guns, and she served for some time with singles in place of the planned twin mounts.

Project 48 would have included as many as fourteen ships, though only ten names appear in records, and not all of these are certain. At least three ships began building, but after a reassessment of the role of the destroyers in general and anti-aircraft defenses in particular, work proceeded on only two. These were evacuated ahead of the German advance, and they lingered incomplete to the mid 1950s before being expended in tests. The collapse of Project 48 canceled hopes of assessing the design in harsher environments, but *Tashkent* performed well during her short career and may rank as the finest fleet unit in Soviet wartime service.

Tashkent *running trials. Her gun and torpedo installations were Soviet responsibilities.*

Production problems with the twin 130mm B-2LM turrets caused Tashkent *to start her career with three single 130mm B-13 guns. The twin turrets and automatic AA guns became available just before the War started.*

Tashkent *was one of the best-looking ships of the Soviet Navy, dubbed "Blue Cruiser" because of her large size and unusual Italian paint scheme.*

Tashkent *evacuating personnel from Sevastopol in 1942. This view shows the central anti-aircraft platform around the aft funnel; this concentration of the light AA guns meant they could all be disabled by a single hit. On the left side of the photo is part of the gunnery control system.*

Tashkent *bringing supplies to Sevastopol in 1942. As one of the fastest ships in the fleet, she made numerous runs into the city, delivering troops and equipment and removing civilians and wounded. On her final run, she brought out 2100 wounded from the besieged city.*

The end came on 2 July 1942 in a surprise raid by sixty-four German bombers. Among the victims was Tashkent, *hit by two bombs. She sank, but her superstructure remained above water, facilitating recovery of important equipment like her twin 130mm turrets and AA guns.*

OPYTNYI class, Project 45

Ship	Builder	Laid Down	Launched	Completed
Opytnyi (ex-*Sergo Ordzhonikidze*)	#190 Zhdanov Yard, Leningrad	26 Jun 35	8 Dec 35	11 Sep 41

Characteristics: 2016 tons full, 113.5 oa x 10.2 x 3.2m, 35 knots, 1370 nm at 18 knots, three 130mm/50, five 45mm/46, two 12.7mm mg, eight 533mm torpedo tubes, 60 mines, 262 men

This experimental unit, cast as the prototype for an entire line of construction, became the most obvious failure of Soviet warship production. The power plant with its new boiler design produced 35 knots instead of the intended 42. Weight-saving measures placed undue reliance on the fledgling art of welding, and the hull turned out to be hopelessly fragile, unable to support the three intended twin 130mm mounts. *Opytnyi* ended up with three single mounts instead but was still too delicate for operations under steam. In the end, she served as a floating artillery platform.

However disappointing Opytnyi *was, she could still perform the primary duty of ships caught in the Leningrad siege. Here she greets German troops in 1942.*

STOROZHEVOI class, Project 7U

Ship	Builder	Laid Down	Launched	Completed
Storozhevoi	#190 Zhdanov Yard, Leningrad	26 Aug 36	2 Oct 38	6 Oct 40
Sil'nyi	#190 Zhdanov Yard, Leningrad	26 Oct 36	1 Nov 38	31 Oct 40
Surovyi (ex-*Letuchii*)	#189 Ordzhonikidze Yard, Leningrad	27 Oct 36	5 Aug 39	31 May 41
Serdityi (ex-*Lihoi*)	#189 Ordzhonikidze Yard, Leningrad	27 Oct 36	21 Apr 39	15 Oct 40
Smelyi	#190 Zhdanov Yard, Leningrad	26 Oct 36	30 Apr 39	31 May 41
Vitse-Admiral Drozd (ex-*Stoikiy*)	#190 Zhdanov Yard, Leningrad	26 Aug 36	26 Dec 38	18 Oct 40
Slavnyi	#189 Ordzhonikidze Yard, Leningrad	31 Aug 36	19 Sep 39	31 May 41

Strashnyi	#190 Zhdanov Yard, Leningrad	26 Aug 36	8 Apr 39	22 Jun 41
Skoryi	#190 Zhdanov Yard, Leningrad	29 Nov 36	24 Jul 39	1 Aug 41
Statnyi	#190 Zhdanov Yard, Leningrad	26 Dec 36	24 Nov 39	18 Jul 41
Svirepyi	#190 Zhdanov Yard, Leningrad	29 Nov 36	28 Aug 39	18 Jul 41
Strogii	#190 Zhdanov Yard, Leningrad	26 Oct 36	31 Dec 39	22 Sep 42
Stroynyi	#190 Zhdanov Yard, Leningrad	26 Dec 36	29 Apr 40	22 Sep 42
Smyshlennyi (ex-*Poleznyi*)	#200 61 Kommunar, Nikolayev	15 Oct 36	26 Aug 39	10 Nov 40
Soobrazitel'nyi (ex-*Prozorlivyi*)	#200 61 Kommunar, Nikolayev	15 Oct 36	26 Aug 39	7 Jun 41
Sposobnyi (ex-*Podvizhyi*)	#200 61 Kommunar, Nikolayev	7 Jul 36	30 Sep 39	24 Jun 41
Svobodnyi (ex-*Besshumnyi*)	#200 61 Kommunar, Nikolayev	23 Aug 36	25 Feb 39	2 Jan 42
Sovershennyi (ex-*Besstrashyi*)	#200 61 Kommunar, Nikolayev	17 Sep 36	25 Feb 39	30 Sep 41

Characteristics: 2337 tons full, 112.5 oa x 10.2 x 4.2m, 36-38 knots, 1680nm at 15 knots, four 130mm/50, two 76.2mm, three 45mm/46, four 12.7mm mg, six 533mm torpedo tubes, 62 mines, 273 men

During the Spanish Civil War, the British destroyer *Hunter* ran onto a mine that left her dead in the water. Like most of the world's destroyers, *Hunter* had her boilers grouped together in the hull forward of the engine rooms. Machinery arrangement had provided lengthy debate as the Soviet destroyer program got underway, but Project 7 repeated *Maestrale*'s conventional layout. Advocates of the unit arrangement of alternating boilers and engines saw the *Hunter* incident as cause to reopen the debate. Stalin himself, always interested in the destroyers, came down – heavily – in favor of the unit arrangement. The folks responsible for the Project 7 machinery found themselves labeled "wreckers."

This had an immediate effect on the *Gnevnyi*s, none of which had reached completion at the time. Stalin demanded rebuilding of the fourteen ships already launched and scrapping of the rest, but the commissar in charge of warship production advised moderation lest the entire destroyer program stall. In the end, the most advanced units continued to Project 7 completion, six of the least complete units were canceled, and eighteen underwent conversion with unit machinery and the new Project 7U title.

Making this fundamental change within the same hull length was a remarkable achievement. Naturally it came with consequences, as in a cramping of the crew spaces and a reduction of range. There were also miscalculations; an expected 60-ton weight gain for the new ships ended up in the hundreds of tons. Figures showed the initial stability, as measured in metacentric height, would drop by 11%, but this turned into a real-world 30%. Adding 100-120 tons of ballast restored some stability but also aggravated the overweight.

Project 7U cost the Soviets several partially complete hulls and many wasted man-hours. This investment yielded little benefit as only once during the war did the unit arrangement save a ship from losing power.

A Project 7U destroyer in wartime showing its distinctive silhouette. The bow and the stern look much like a Project 7's, but the midships changed completely with its two stacks.

Slavnyi *in Leningrad, 1945. By war's end, most of the Baltic Project 7U ships featured the extra 76mm 34-K gun on the stern.*

Svobodny *served only six months before her loss on 9 June 1942. After escorting the transport* Abkhaziya *into Sevastopol, she took nine bomb hits. Sixty-seven people died, and the explosion of her ammunition demolished the ship.*

Units in besieged Leningrad resorted to extreme measures in camouflage. Here a Project 7U destroyer wears strips of cloth to break up her silhouette.

Wartime details of the Project 7U aft superstructure, including the blast deflector above the lower gun. In a continuation of Imperial practice, the Soviet Navy often covered railings with canvas to reduce wetness.

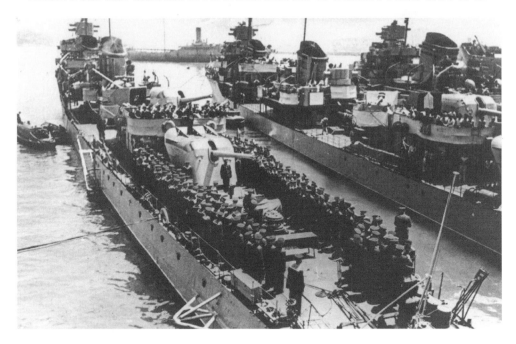

Soobrazitel'nyi, Sposobnyi, *and* Besposhchadnyi *in Batumi, 6 June 1943. The large blast deflectors are gone, replaced by extensions on the lower gun shields.*

Icebound Strogii *in the Neva River firing at the German positions in 1944. Like other ships in Leningrad, she has a unique camouflage scheme.*

Sovershennyi had little luck. Mined while running trials in 1941, she successfully returned to Sevastopol only to suffer bomb damage which caused her to capsize. Salvage operations made progress until German artillery finished her off.

OGNEVOI class, Project 30

Ship	Builder	Laid Down	Launched	Completed
Ognevoi (ex-Opasnyi)	#200 61 Kommunar, Nikolayev	20 Nov 39	Nov 1940	May 1945
Osmotritel'nyi	#402 Factory, Molotovsk	5 May 40	24 Aug 44	28 Oct 47
Vnushitelnyi	#199 Amurski Shipyard, Komsomol'sk-na-Amure	16 Oct 40	1942?	29 Dec 47
Okhotnik	#402 Factory, Molotovsk	25 Jun 40	19 Jul 47	29 Sep 48
Otlichnyi	#190 Zhdanov Yard, Leningrad	2 Dec 39	early 1941	31 Oct 48
Vynoslivyi	#199 Amurski Shipyard, Komsomol'sk-na-Amure	29 Oct 40	17 Nov 47	5 Dec 48
Vlastrnyi	#199 Amurski Shipyard, Komsomol'sk-na-Amure	29 Oct 40	15 Jun 48	27 Dec 48
Ozornoyi	#200 61 Kommunar, Nikolayev	20 Nov 39	25 Dec 40	9 Jan 49

Obraztsovyi	#190 Zhdanov Yard, Leningrad	2 Dec 39	early 1941	29 Sep 49
Otvaznyi	#190 Zhdanov Yard, Leningrad	30 Dec 39	early 1941	2 Mar 50
Odarennyi	#190 Zhdanov Yard, Leningrad	30 Dec 39	27 Dec 48	28 Jun 50
Ognennyi	#190 Zhdanov Yard, Leningrad	1940	—	—
Ozhestochennyi	#190 Zhdanov Yard, Leningrad	1940	—	—
Ostryi	#190 Zhdanov Yard, Leningrad	1940	—	—
Oslepitelnyi	#190 Zhdanov Yard, Leningrad	1940	—	—
Ostorozhnyi	#190 Zhdanov Yard, Leningrad	1941	—	—
Otchetlivyi	#190 Zhdanov Yard, Leningrad	1941	—	—
Otmennyi	#200 61 Kommunar, Nikolayev	1940	—	—
Obuchennyi	#200 61 Kommunar, Nikolayev	1940	—	—
Otchayannyi	#200 61 Kommunar, Nikolayev	1940	—	—
Obshitelnyi	#200 61 Kommunar, Nikolayev	1940	—	—
Organizovannyi	#189 Ordzhnikidze Yard, Leningrad	1941	—	—
Otbornyi	#189 Ordzhnikidze Yard, Leningrad	Apr 1941	—	—
Otrazhayuschii	#189 Ordzhnikidze Yard, Leningrad	Apr 1941	—	—
Zharkii	#402 Factory, Molotovsk	25 Mar 41	—	—
Zhivoi	#402 Factory, Molotovsk	25 Mar 41	—	—
Zhestkii	#402 Factory, Molotovsk	25 Mar 41	—	—
Veduschii	#199 Amurski Shipyard, Komsomol'sk-na-Amure	22 Sep 41	—	—

Vnezapnyi	#199 Amurski Shipyard, Komsomol'sk-na-Amure	22 Sep 41	—	—
Zhutkii	#402 Factory, Molotovsk	1941	—	—
Otradnyi	#190 Zhdanov Yard, Leningrad	—	—	—
Ozhivlennyi	#190 Zhdanov Yard, Leningrad	—	—	—
Otlichitel'nyi	#190 Zhdanov Yard, Leningrad	—	—	—
Zhestokii	#402 Factory, Molotovsk	—	—	—
Zorkii	#402 Factory, Molotovsk	—	—	—
Zvonkii	#402 Factory, Molotovsk	—	—	—

Characteristics: 2767 tons full, 115.5 oa x 11 x 4.6m, 37 knots, 2400 nm at 16 knots, four 130mm/50, two 76.2mm/55, six 37mm/67, four 12.7mm mgs, six 533mm torpedo tubes, 60 mines, 293 men

Ognevoi had a different look compared to the Project 7/7U destroyers, with her twin turrets and enlarged superstructure. The enclosed turrets represented a comfortable and practical improvement over shielded mounts, but they lacked high elevation. The major fleets – American, British, and Japanese – all mounted DP guns on destroyers during the war, leaving the Soviets to play catch-up.

Ognevoi's *aft twin 130mm B-2LM turret entered service four years before she did, having originally been aboard* Tashkent. *The twin 76mm 39-K turret is visible above it. Tarps cover the six 37mm 70-K cannon (four beside the aft stack and two abreast the forward superstructure).*

Derived from Project 7U, *Ognevoi* enjoyed a set of significant improvements. Mounting the main battery in twin turrets increased stability. The hull form remained similar enough for incomplete *Organizovannyi* to donate her bow for repair of the Project 7U *Storozhevoi*, resulting in a unique Project 7U/30 ship.

The tumult of war delayed construction so that only *Ognevoi* herself was commissioned by 1945. Her sisters became subject of enough tinkering to be relabeled as Project 30K. The original provision for 76mm AA guns gave way to more capable 85mm guns. These ships formed the basis for the Soviet Union's first postwar destroyer classes.

American "Flushdeckers"

Ship	Builder	Laid Down	Launched	Completed
Wickes class				
Zhivuchiy (ex-*Fairfax*, ex-*Richmond*)	Mare Island Navy Yard	10 Jul 17	15 Dec 17	6 Apr 18

Zhguchiy (ex-Twiggs, ex-Leamington)	New York Shipbuilding, Camden	23 Jan 18	28 Sep 18	28 Jul 19
Derzkiy (ex-Crown-inshield, ex-Chelsea)	Bath Iron Works	5 Nov 18	24 Jul 19	6 Aug 19
Druzhnyi (ex-Yarnall, ex-Lincoln)	Cramp Shipyard	12 Feb 18	19 Jun 18	29 Nov 18
Zharkiy (ex-Cowell, ex-Brighton)	Fore River, Quincy	15 Jul 18	23 Nov 18	17 Mar 19
Zhestkiy (ex-Maddox, ex-Georgetown)	Fore River, Quincy	20 Jul 18	27 Oct 18	10 Mar 19
Doblestnyi (ex-Foote, ex-Roxborough)	Fore River, Quincy	7 Aug 18	14 Dec 18	21 Mar 19
Dostoinyi (ex-Thomas, ex-St. Albans)	Newport News	23 Mar 18	4 Jul 18	25 Apr 19
Clemson class				
Deyatelnyi (ex-Herndon, ex-Churchill)	Newport News	25 Nov 18	31 May 19	14 Sep 20

Characteristics: 1552 tons full, 95.6 x 9.42 x 3.56m, 27 knots, 1900 nm at 15 knots, one 102mm, one 76mm, six 20mm, three 533mm torpedo tubes, 141 men

The American system of naval appropriations subjected the fleet to the whims of Congress, and Congress had duly whimsically opted not to give the fleet any scouts. Seeing that politicians would authorize destroyers more readily than cruisers, the navy decided on the desperate measure of tailoring its destroyer designs for scouting duty. At one third the size of the 1908 Chesters (the last cruiser class to enter service), the resulting ships could not hope to give cruiser-like performance, but they were nonetheless sizeable by destroyer standards. The navy took comfort in knowing that size would help with traditional destroyers duties as well. Authorized in 1915, the Caldwell class of six prototypes was built with a strong flushdeck hull and a variety of propulsion plants.

The winds of wartime whimsy then blessed the navy with an order for three scout designs all at once: the Lexington-class battlecruisers, the Omaha-class light cruisers, and the big destroyers. The cruisers, designed with no immediate predecessors, turned out to be dreadful, but the destroyers inherited Caldwell's virtues and gained powerful new machinery. The initial order turned into an unprecedented mass-production effort split into two groups, the Clemson and

Wickes classes. The war emergency forced construction into a large number of yards and thus produced more than the usual variation, especially in propulsion. It also precluded adoption of modern features, and the ships entered service already outdated.

The flushdeckers came into Soviet service by a circuitous route. President Roosevelt traded fifty units to Britain in 1940 to provide trans-oceanic escort. Despite extensive conversion for this role, the elderly ships became less valuable as they wore out and as new, dedicated anti-submarine designs entered service. A few units transferred temporarily to Norwegian crews. When the time came to placate Stalin in his thirst for Italian war booty, the flushdeckers became obvious candidates, serving with the Soviets for five years until replaced in 1949 by the ex-Italian *Fuciliere* and *Artigliere*.

Romanian *VIFOR* class

Ship	Builder	Laid Down	Launched	Completed
Lovkiy (ex-*Vijelie*, ex-*Sparviero*, ex-*Mărăşti*)	Pattison, Naples	29 Jan 14	25 Mar 17	15 Jul 17
Legkiy (ex-*Vârtej*, ex-*Nibbio*, ex-*Mărăşeşti*)	Pattison, Naples	15 Jul 14	30 Jan 18	15 May 18

Characteristics: 1723 tons full, 94.3 oa x 9.45 x 3.51m, 34 knots, 1026nm at 15 knots, four 120mm/45, two 37mm, five 20mm, four 13.2mm mg, four 450mm torpedo tubes, 50 mines, 241 men

Like the flushdeckers, *Mărăşti* and *Mărăşeşti* joined the Soviets only after a wide-ranging journey. It began with Romania's 1912 plan for dramatic naval expansion including six 3500-ton light cruisers and a dozen large destroyers. Almost the entire plan fell through except for four destroyers ordered from an Italian yard. Pattison had made a name for itself building torpedo boats and destroyers for the Italian navy, working at first with foreign firms like Thornycroft but eventually producing its own successful designs. The Romanians provided specifications for a 1500-ton ship, and Pattison produced a suitable interpretation. Unfortunately, construction began shortly before the outbreak of World War I, and the Italian navy seized all four ships. Though two of them remained in Italian service until transferred to Spain in the 1930s, the Romanians recovered the other pair in 1920 and gave them new names to commemorate recent battles. The Soviets took both in August 1944 and returned them two years later.

Unlike many of the ships involved in the 1940 destroyers-for-bases trade, Zharkiy *retained four funnels and the general look of the original flushdecker design.*

Mărăşti *as seen from* Regina Maria *in June 1941. Extremely powerful when ordered, still useful thirty years later, she lingered as a training ship before her scrapping in the 1960s. – courtesy of Modelism.*

Likhoi *looks very British, but without the electronics that every British destroyer would have carried at this time.*

Romanian *REGELE FERDINAND* class

Ship	Builder	Laid Down	Launched	Completed
Likhoi (ex-*Regele Ferdinand*)	Pattison, Naples	Jun 1927	2 Dec 28	7 Sep 30
Letuchyi (ex-*Regina Maria*)	Pattison, Naples	Jun 1927	2 Mar 29	7 Sep 30

Characteristics: 2320 tons full load, 101.9 oa x 9.6 x 3.5m, 35 knots, 2750nm at 13 knots, four 120mm/50, one 88mm, three 37mm, two 20mm, two 13.2mm mg, six 533mm torpedo tubes, 50 mines, 241 men

After World War I, the Romanians returned to Pattison for another four destroyers, but once again the navy received only two ships, this time due to finances. (This proved equally woeful for the builder, whose warship business dried up shortly after this order.) Pattison's British connection came through with a Thornycroft design similar to Britain's *Shakespeare*-class flotilla leader. This gave the Romanians another powerful class, in this case improved from the original by the adoption of a unit machinery arrangement.

All four Romanian destroyers fell under Soviet control at the same time. The modern pair remained there into the 1950s before returning and were discarded in the 1960s.

CHAPTER 4

Submarines

The submarine fit in well with ideology-driven naval policies, and the demands of construction were easy enough to allow an early resumption of submarine projects. Consequently, the Soviets went into World War II with a submarine fleet that outnumbered the combined fleets of the two nearest rivals.

These massive numbers didn't translate into wartime success. The boats themselves, while not incapable, fell somewhat below foreign standards in design, workmanship, and materials. Nevertheless, the horrific successes late in World War II illustrated a distinct potential. What negated the Soviet submarine threat for so much of the war was a set of obstacles quite unlike anything that any foreign service had to face. Barbarossa swallowed base facilities. Harsh weather and logistical difficulties limited training. The Baltic offered significant opportunities, but the Germans – otherwise miserable at combatting subs – cordoned off their enemy behind a nearly impenetrable mine barrage. From December 1942 to September 1944, Soviet Baltic submarines managed perhaps five attacks and sank nothing.

The list of frustrations can mask the degree to which the Soviets channeled their innovative spirit into submarines, a natural holdover from tsarist days. Propulsion experiments received close attention. Miniatures became the vogue. A pair of 8-ton midgets were built in 1936 but apparently provoked little interest despite a suggested adaptation into unmanned explosive craft. The Bloha type, effectively a submersible MTB, reached its end as a prototype, 60% complete when Barbarossa ended the work.

M-171 *(ex-M-87) began as a standard Series XII submarine. She mounted one of the first SPRUT-1 devices intended for maintaining position when submerged. In 1943 she made history with the first torpedo attack based entirely on acoustics. The following year, she underwent conversion with bulges for eighteen mines. The minelaying system worked well enough, but the project fizzled, leaving* M-171 *a portly one-off.*

Opposite above: Pigmey, *one of the midget proposals, would carry two torpedoes, one in the slot on each side of the hull. The Germans captured and photographed the prototype in Sevastopol in 1942.*

Opposite below: *A rare view of* M-401, *an experimental variant of the Series XII. Completed in 1942, she spent the war on the Caspian conducting trials with her closed-cycle diesel propulsion – a relatively successful experiment, but too complex for mass production.*

BARS class

Ship	Builder	Laid Down	Launched	Completed
B-1 (ex-*Tigr*, ex-*No. 1*, ex-*Kommunar*, ex-*No. 11*)	Nobel & Lessner, Reval	3 Jul 13	5 Sep 15	14 Apr 16
B-2 (ex-*Pantera*, ex-*No. 5*, ex-*Komissar*, ex-*No. 13*)	Nobel & Lessner, Reval	3 Jul 14	14 Apr 16	23 Jul 16
B-3 (ex-*Rys'*, ex-*Bol'shevik*)	Nobel & Lessner, Reval	3 Jul 14	Jul 1916	7 Nov 17
B-4 (ex-*Yaguar*, ex-*No. 8*, ex-*Krasnoflotets*, ex-*No. 22*)	Nobel & Lessner, Reval	3 Jul 14	Nov 1916	12 Oct 17
B-5 (ex-*Volk*, ex-*No. 2*, ex-*Batrak*, ex-*No. 21*, ex-*U-1*)	Baltic Factory, St. Petersburg	15 Sep 13	25 Oct 15	14 Apr 16
B-6 (ex-*Zmeya*, ex-*No. 6*, ex-*Proletarii*, ex-*No. 23*, ex-*U-3*)	Baltic Factory, St. Petersburg	1915	Nov 1916	27 Mar 17
B-7 (ex-*Leopard*, ex-*No. 4*, ex-*Krasnoflotets*, ex-*No. 24*, ex*U2*)	Nobel & Lessner, Reval	3 Jul 14	10 Oct 15	10 Jun 16
B-8 (ex-*Tyr*, ex-*No. 3*, ex*Tovarisch*, ex-*No. 12*)	Nobel & Lessner, Reval	3 Jul 14	20 May 16	8 Aug 17
Rabochiy (ex-*Yorsh*, ex-*No. 9*)	Nobel & Lessner, Reval	3 Jul 14	May 1917	15 Dec 17
Bednyak (ex-*Kuguar*, ex-*No. 10*)	Nobel & Lessner, Reval	3 Jul 14	1916	22 Dec 16

Characteristics: 650-670/780-810 tons, 68 oa x 4.5 x 4.12m, 9.7-12.5/7.8-9 knots, 1900nm-2500nm at cruising speed/30nm at cruising speed, two 75mm/50, one 7.62mm mg, four 450mm torpedo tubes and eight torpedo cradles, 34 men

The *Bars* project, originally including twenty-four boats, formed around the concept of a submarine that could act in close coordination with the surface fleet (a bad idea that afflicted most major navies at some point or other). This dictated a requirement for high speed, and the *Bars* design indeed achieved excellent speed, even if the boats themselves did not. A hoped-for partnership with Krupp for diesel production evaporated with the start of World War I, so only *Kuguar* and *Zmeya* received the intended power plant – a mixed blessing for them, as the big diesels proved unreliable and difficult to service.

The design developed from the *Morzh* class and likewise featured torpedo cradles, popular in Russia because they provided a unique ability to fire large salvos. However, mounted externally on the hull, they exposed the torpedoes to battle damage, freezing, water pressure, and other hazards. They also interfered with the boat's speed, and surviving units had them removed.

Unfortunately, two more fundamental flaws – an absence of watertight bulkheads and a painfully long dive time – remained beyond correction. Never a success, these boats were significant for the simple reason that they existed when the Soviets had few others in service.

Right: Kommunar *in the 1920s without her Drzewiecki torpedo cradles. In giving these boats a 3-minute dive time and no effective subdivision, the Russians assured them a rapid obsolescence. Only B-2 remained on the navy rolls into 1940.*

Below: Yorsh, *one of two units built as minelayers. She had two mine tubes in the aft section of the upper hull and only one deck gun.*

"AG" class

Ship	Builder	Laid Down	Launched	Completed
A-1 (ex-AG-23, ex-AG-23 Imeni Tovarishcha Trotskogo, ex-PL-16, ex-Nezamozhyi, ex-Shakhter No. 12)	Russud, Nikolayev	May 1917	1 Jun 20	21 Oct 20
A-2 (ex-AG-24, ex-AG-24 Imeni Tovarischa Lunacharskogo, ex-PL-17, ex-Kommunist No. 13)	Russud, Nikolayev	1 Jun 20	7 Apr 21	22 Jul 21
A-3 (ex-AG-25, ex-PL-18, ex-Marksist No. 14)	Russud, Nikolayev	11 Jul 21	5 Apr 22	26 May 22
A-4 (ex-AG-26, ex-AG-26 Imeni Tovarischa Kameneva, ex-PL-19, ex-Politrabotnik No. 15)	Russud, Nikolayev	23 Oct 20	24 Feb 23	11 Jul 23
A-5 (ex-AG-21, ex-Metallist No. 16)	Russud, Nikolayev	1917	1917	1918

Characteristics: 360/470 tons normal, 47.5 oa x 4.88 x 2.7m, 13/8 knots, 1750 nm at 8 knots, one 45mm 21-K, four 450mm torpedo tubes, 32 men

This Holland design from America (AG = Amerikanski Golland) saw service in at least seven navies, establishing a long and successful career. The Russians ordered seventeen units, prefabricated in North America to be reassembled in Russia. Politics, war, and revolution left only five available for Soviet service.

British "L" class

Ship	Builder	Laid Down	Launched	Completed
L-55	Fairfield, Glasgow	May 1917	21 Sep 18	19 Dec 18

Characteristics: 954/1139 tons, 72 oa x 7.2 x 4.1m, 13.9/9 knots, 5550nm at 7.4 knots/100nm at 2.9 knots, two 76.2mm, six bow 533mm torpedo tubes, twelve torpedoes, 56 men

During the Intervention in 1919, the British L-55 struck a mine while engaging Red destroyers. Deleting the mine reference allowed publicized accounts to credit Azard with a heroic victory over capitalist submariners.

Seven years later, after a trawler happened to recover a British gunsight, the Soviets realized they had an opportunity to examine a relatively modern foreign design. With domestic construction about to resume, it was decided to

No. 12 Shakhter *in the Black Sea as configured in the late 1920s.*

A-5 *just before the war showing her final modernization with built-up superstructure and 45mm 21-K AA gun.*

salvage *L-55*. The submarine salvage ship *Kommuna* brought the wreck to the surface in August 1928, and the Soviets had their prize.

Not content with mere examination, the navy resolved to rebuild and recommission *L-55*. With work completed on 7 August 1931, the boat began trials. These proved dramatic when the boat plummeted to the bottom; her rapid-diving tanks were a feature unfamiliar to the Soviets. *L-55* officially entered Soviet service on 5 October 1931 under her original name.

Detailed study of the British boat yielded numerous lessons, and her significance lies in her influence on subsequent design rather than in her own operational career. She served in training until classified as an experimental vessel in 1940, demoted soon after to a mobile charging plant under the designation *PZS-2*. She recovered her name postwar and lasted into the 1950s.

Artwork by N. Bublikov depicting Azard *and* Gavriil *and the destruction by gunfire of the British L-55. The Bolsheviks found more to celebrate in this fiction than in the truth that the sub accidentally ran into a British minefield.*

Opposite above:*The wrecked remnant of L-55's fairwater as she sits in drydock awaiting repairs.*

Above and below: L-55 *kept her name in the Soviet service; she even kept her Latin "L," at least initially. The main identifying feature was the oversized fairwater mounting two 76mm guns.*

"D" Class, Series I

Ship	Builder	Laid Down	Launched	Completed
D-1 (ex-*Dekabrist*)	Ordzhonikidze, Leningrad	5 Mar 27	3 Nov 28	12 Nov 30
D-2 (ex-*Narodovolyets*)	Ordzhonikidze, Leningrad	5 Mar 27	19 May 29	6 Sep 31
D-3 (ex-*Krasnogvardyets*)	Ordzhonikidze, Leningrad	5 Mar 27	12 Jul 29	1 Oct 31
D-4 (ex-*Revolyutsioner*)	Marti Yard, Nikolayev	14 Apr 27	16 Apr 29	30 Dec 31
D-5 (ex-*Spartakovets*)	Marti Yard, Nikolayev	14 Apr 27	28 Sep 29	5 May 31
D-6 (ex-*Yakobinets*)	Marti Yard, Nikolayev	14 Apr 27	12 May 30	15 Jun 31

Characteristics: 934/1361 tons, 76.6 oa x 6.4 x 3.81m, 14.6/8.5 knots, 8950nm at 9 knots/158nm at 2.9 knots, one 100mm/51, one 45mm/46, one 7.62mm mg, six bow + two stern 533mm torpedo tubes, 53 men

The Soviets began generating requirements for a renewed submarine arm as early as 1923, but the specifics of design and industrial limitation kept the matter in limbo. A proposed continuation of the *Bars* program earned little support, given the type's obvious inferiority. In 1925, things started to happen. A mission to Italy managed to acquire drawings for the brand-new *Ballila* class. Overtures to Germany were not so immediately fruitful, but within a year the Germans provided plans to four of their World War I designs. By the end of 1926, the Soviets ordered their first new submarines.

The navy hoped for its submarine design bureau to advance by leaps and bounds to catch up with foreign standards, but *Dekabrist* was clearly a baby-step. Though of double-hulled type, the design called for streamlining the internal pressure hull. Inadequate weight disciplines created a 10-ton excess. Parroting a feature from *Ballila*, designers included a structure they guessed was meant to help maintain periscope depth, only later learning that it was a tank for rapid diving; the "D" design was nearly complete before *L-55* taught its lessons.

The boats were quick to exhibit their family of bugs, and yet the problems were no greater than might be expected from such a ground-breaking project. Experience prompted a series of remedial alterations, and if the *Dekabrist*s never became war-winners, they at least achieved mediocrity and provided a sound footing for the nascent submarine program.

For D-4, seen here in the Black Sea in 1935, the salient feature was the 102mm gun mounted forward on the large fairwater.

The Northern Fleet's D-3 in wartime. As modernized, the subs could easily be confused with the "L" class, but the main distinguishing feature remained the large, folding bow planes.

D-2 in Leningrad postwar after all modernizations. A deck-level 100mm B-24 submarine gun has replaced the 102mm gun on the fairwater. The fairwater itself has more conventional contours.

"L" class, Series II

Ship	Builder	Laid Down	Launched	Completed
L-1 (ex-*Leninets*)	Ordzhonikidze, Leningrad	6 Sep 29	28 Feb 31	22 Oct 33
L-2 (ex-*Stalinets*, ex-*Marksist*)	Ordzhonikidze, Leningrad	6 Sep 29	21 May 31	24 Oct 33
L-3 (ex-*Frunzevets*, ex-*Bolshevik*)	Ordzhonikidze, Leningrad	6 Sep 29	8 Jul 31	5 Nov 33
L-4 (ex-*Garibaldiets*)	Marti Yard, Nikolayev	15 Mar 30	31 Aug 31	8 Oct 33
L-5 (ex-*Chartist*)	Marti Yard, Nikolayev	15 Mar 30	5 Jun 32	30 Oct 33
L-6 (ex-*Karbonari*)	Marti Yard, Nikolayev	15 Apr 30	3 Nov 32	5 Sep 33

Characteristics: 1025/1312 tons, 78 oa x 7.2 x 3.96m, 14.2/8.5 knots, 7400nm at 9 knots/154nm at 2.5 knots, one 100mm/51, one 45mm/46, six bow 533mm torpedo tubes, 55 men

The Soviets saw submarines as the premier minelaying vehicle. The first "L" class, an offshoot of the "D" design with extensive reference to *L-55*, sacrificed a stern torpedo armament in favor of two horizontal mine tubes. The boats demanded high maintenance but proved sufficiently convincing to warrant three follow-on series.

An "L" shows the light paint scheme used for Black Sea subs in the 1930s.

L-4 gives a good view of the large tubes, which each carried ten PLT mines.

The "L" class out-sizes the "Shch" class in Tallin, 1940.

Black Sea boat L-4 *showing the turreted 100mm gun common in early units.*

A German transport rammed L-3 on 13 November 1942.

"Shch" class, Series III (also known as *Shchuka* class)

Ship	Builder	Laid Down	Launched	Completed
Shch-301 (ex-*Shchuka*)	#189 Factory, Ordzhonikidze, Leningrad	5 Feb 30	1 Dec 30	11 Oct 33
Shch-302 (ex-*kun*)	#189 Factory, Ordzhonikidze, Leningrad	5 Feb 30	6 Nov 31	11 Oct 33
Shch-303 (ex-*Yorsh*)	#189 Factory, Ordzhonikidze, Leningrad	5 Feb 30	6 Nov 31	15 Nov 33
Shch-304 (ex-*Komsomolets*, ex-*Yaz'*, ex-*Udarnik*)	#112 Factory, Krasnoe Sormovo, Gorky	23 Feb 30	2 May 31	15 Aug 34

Characteristics: 572/672 tons, 57 oa x 6.2 x 3.76m, 11.6/8.5 knots, 3130nm at 8.5 knots/112nm at 2.8 knots, one 45mm/46, two 7.62mm mgs, four bow + two stern 533mm torpedo tubes, 40 men

Decision-makers saw such urgency in this project that they initiated construction before designers had finalized their work. This necessitated some

Three of the first four Shchukas in the 1930s. Note the folding sides of the gun platform and a large door in the fairwater.

frenetic redistribution of weights, but *Shchuka* fathered a well-liked lineage that eventually became the most numerous among Soviet subs.

The first series illustrated that designers had not yet mastered some details in watertightness, but there were no catastrophes. It proved impractical to fire more than two forward tubes in a salvo owing to effects on trim.

Shch-304 was a late addition to the class, paid for by public subscription. Launched at Gorky, she transferred to the #189 Factory for completion. These boats began with fish names in accordance with Russian tradition, then switched over to numbers before completion.

Shch-303 Yorsh
docking at
Kronshtadt c1942.
The first "Shch"
class is recognizable
by its straight stem.

"P" class, Series IV

Ship	Builder	Laid Down	Launched	Completed
P-1 (ex-*Pravda*)	Ordzhonikidze, Leningrad	21 May 31	3 Jan 34	9 Jun 36
P-2 (ex-*Zvezda*)	Ordzhonikidze, Leningrad	19 Dec 31	15 Feb 34	9 Jul 36
P-3 (ex-*Iskra*)	Ordzhonikidze, Leningrad	19 Dec 31	4 Dec 34	9 Jul 36
P-4?	Ordzhonikidze, Leningrad	—	—	—

Characteristics: 931/1685 ton, 87.7 oa x 8.0 x 2.9m, 20.2/8.3 knots, 5535nm at 10.9 knots/96nm at 4.1 knots,
two 102/45, one 45mm/46, four bow + two stern 533mm torpedo tubes, 53-56 men

In 1931, France completed *Redoutable*, its first "fleet" submarine intended for close coordination with the battle fleet. The British laid down their first "River" class boats for the same purpose. In America, the transition had begun between the big "V" type cruiser subs and the leaner design with their high speed to allow operations with surface units. Japan was well into its program of fast, brawny I-boats.

In this context, the Soviet decision to revisit the fleet-boat concept is no surprise. Unfortunately, the tug-of-war that characterized Soviet design bureaucracy had an especially gruesome effect on the "P" design, making it, by far, the least successful Soviet submarine of this period.

Once again, construction began with the design still unfinished. When the surface speed requirement inspired a hull design reminiscent of a destroyer's, it was left to the completed boats to show the consequences. They handled poorly when submerged and on the surface. Waves lifted their screws completely out of the water. A late realization of hull weakness sent designers scrambling for modification. This proved successful, at a significant cost in tonnage, which necessitated some dramatic weight-cutting. The design thus had its gun armament reduced and lost part of its propulsion plant, shaving three knots off the surface speed. Series VI became a dead end, with all three units classified as training subs as soon as they commissioned. War service included transport and early retirement.

P-3. *The intended armament of two 130mm/45 guns became two 102mm/45 guns. The batteries required 20 hours of recharging.*

Navy Day festivities in Leningrad.

"Shch" class, Series V (also known as "Shchuka-A" class)

Ship	Builder	Laid Down	Launched	Completed
Shch-101 (ex-*Losos*, ex-*No. 11*)	#189 Factory, Ordzhonikidze, Leningrad	20 Mar 32	25 Dec 32	22 Sep 33
Shch-102 (ex-*Lesch*, ex-*No. 12*)	#189 Factory, Ordzhonikidze; #194 Factory Marti, Leningrad	20 Mar 32	19 Apr 33	22 Sep 33
Shch-103 (ex-*Karp*, ex-*No. 13*)	#189 Factory, Ordzhonikidze; #194 Factory Marti, Leningrad	20 Mar 32	May 1933	27 Oct 33
Shch-104 (ex-*Nalim*, ex-*No. 14*)	#189 Factory, Ordzhonikidze, Leningrad	20 Mar 32	May 1933	5 Nov 33
Shch-105 (ex-*Keta*, ex-*No. 21*)	#189 Factory, Ordzhonikidze, Leningrad	1 Apr 32	Aug 1933	5 Nov 33
Shch-106 (ex-*Sudak*, ex-*No. 22*)	#189 Factory, Ordzhonikidze; #190 Factory Zhdanov, Leningrad	27 Mar 32	May 1933	20 Nov 33

Shch-107 (ex-*Sig*, ex-*No. 23*)	#189 Factory, Ordzhonikidze; #190 Factory Zhdanov, Leningrad	27 Mar 32	Jul 1933	27 Nov 33
Shch-108 (ex-*Forel'*, ex-*No. 24*)	#189 Factory, Ordzhonikidze, Leningrad	1 Apr 32	Aug 33	21 Dec 33
Shch-109 (ex-*Som*, ex-*No. 31*)	#189 Factory, Ordzhonikidze; #190 Factory Zhdanov, Leningrad	20 Mar 32	Aug 1933	18 Apr 34
Shch-110 (ex-*Yaz'*, ex-*No. 32*)	#189 Factory, Ordzhonikidze; #190 Factory Zhdanov, Leningrad	20 Mar 32	Oct 1933	18 May 34
Shch-111 (ex-*Karas'*, ex-*No. 33*)	#189 Factory, Ordzhonikidze, Leningrad	20 Mar 32	Jul 1933	11 Sep 34
Shch-112 (ex-*Peskar'*)	#189 Factory, Ordzhonikidze, Leningrad	20 Mar 32	Apr 1934	11 Sep 34

Characteristics: 592/715 tons, 58.5 oa x 6.2 x 3.79m, 11.9/8.5 knots, 4500nm at 8.5 knots/100nm at 2.8 knots, two 45mm/46, two 7.62mm mgs, four bow + two stern 533mm torpedo tubes; ten torpedoes, 40 men

The second of six *Shchuka* classes made minor improvements on the original, replacing the straight stem and incorporating various hull refinements. The torpedo-induced trim problems continued, as did the fish-name/number changing. All units were transported to the Far East for final assembly.

A Pacific Fleet Shchuka. *Unlike Series III, Series V featured two 45mm guns, a stepped superstructure, and an angled stem.*

Above and below: *A Pacific base, 1945. A 12.7mm DShK machine gun has displaced the after 45mm gun, a weapon considered inadequate for most roles – too weak to sink surface ships and hopeless against aircraft. The inscription on the torpedo says, "Death to the Samurais."*

"Shch" class, Series V-bis (also known as "Shchuka-A" class)

Ship	Builder	Laid Down	Launched	Completed
Shch-113 (ex-Sterlyad')	#194 Factory Marti, Leningrad	10 Oct 32	12 Dec 33	11 Sep 34
Shch-114 (ex-Sevryuga)	#194 Factory Marti, Leningrad	10 Oct 32	early 1934	11 Sep 34
Shch-115 (ex-Skat)	#189 Factory, Ordzhonikidze, Leningrad	19 Oct 32	4 Apr 34	10 Oct 34
Shch-116 (ex-Osetr)	Ordzhonikidze, Leningrad	12 May 33	early 1934	11 Jan 35
Shch-117 (ex-Makrel')	#189 Factory, Ordzhonikidze, Leningrad	9 Oct 32	15 Apr 34	18 Dec 34
Shch-118 (ex-Kefal')	#189 Factory, Ordzhonikidze, Leningrad	10 Oct 32	early 1934	18 Dec 34
Shch-119 (ex-Beluga)	Ordzhonikidze, Leningrad	12 May 33	7 May 34	2 Feb 35
Shch-120 (ex-Navaga)	#194 Factory Marti, Leningrad	2 Apr 33	Jun 1934	30 Jan 35
Shch-201 (ex-Sazan)	#194 Factory Marti, Leningrad	14 Aug 33	3 Apr 34	5 Aug 35
Shch-202 (ex-Seld')	#194 Factory Marti, Leningrad	3 Sep 33	25 May 34	3 Sep 35
Shch-203 (ex-Kambala)	#189 Factory, Ordzhonikidze, Leningrad	10 Mar 33	29 May 34	4 Sep 35
Shch-305 (ex-Lin', ex-Voinstvuyshchiy Bezbozhnik)	#194 Factory Marti, Leningrad	Nov 1932	31 Dec 33	3 Dec 34
Shch-308 (ex-Semga)	Krasnoe Sormovo, Gorky	10 Nov 32	28 Apr 33	14 Nov 35

Characteristics: 592/716 tons normal, 58.8 oa x 6.2 x 3.94m, 12.3/8.5 knots, 4500nm at 8.5 knots/100nm at 2.5 knots, two 45mm/46, four bow + two stern 533mm torpedo tubes, ten torpedoes, 40 men

A hasty timetable turned a comprehensive refinement of the "Shch" type into a minor modification. As became standard with the type, the 100-numbered boats transferred to the Far East for assembly, and the 200-numbered boats were completed at Nikolayev.

Some Series V-bis boats, like this one in Petropavlovsk-Kamchatski on May Day 1943, were modified with a permanent, railing-enclosed gun platform rather than a folding one.

This Pacific Fleet Series V-bis boat shows the lack of a step between the fairwater and the forward 45mm gun, distinguishing it from the Series V. Note the folding sides of the forward gun platform.

Shch-203 in the Black Sea. The variable angle for the top edge of the fairwater differs from the smoothly sloping line of the later Series V-bis-2.

"Shch" class, Series V-bis-2

Ship	Builder	Laid Down	Launched	Completed
Shch-121 (ex-*Zubatka*)	#194 Factory Marti, Leningrad	20 Dec 33	26 Aug 34	30 Apr 35
Shch-122 (ex-*Saida*)	#189 Factory, Ordzhonikidze, Leningrad	22 Dec 33	29 Aug 34	30 Apr 35
Shch-123 (ex-*Ugor'*)	#194 Factory Marti, Leningrad	20 Dec 33	26 Aug 34	30 Apr 35
Shch-124 (ex-*Paltus*)	#189 Factory, Ordzhonikidze, Leningrad	22 Dec 33	29 Dec 34	29 Sep 35
Shch-125 (ex-*Muksun*)	#194 Factory Marti, Leningrad	20 Dec 33	26 Aug 34	15 May 36
Shch-204 (ex-*Minoga*)	#194 Factory Marti, Leningrad	15 Apr 34	31 Dec 34	30 Dec 35

Shch-205 (ex-Nerpa)	#200 Factory 61 Kommunar yard, Nikolayev	5 Jan 34	6 Nov 34	17 Nov 36
Shch-206 (ex-Nel'ma)	#200 Factory 61 Kommunar yard, Nikolayev	5 Jan 34	1 Feb 35	14 Aug 36
Shch-207 (ex-Kasatka)	#200 Factory 61 Kommunar yard, Nikolayev	5 Jan 34	25 Mar 35	17 Nov 36
Shch-306 (ex-Piksha)	#189 Factory, Ordzhonikidze, Leningrad	6 Nov 33	1 Aug 34	4 Aug 35
Shch-307 (ex-Treska)	#189 Factory, Ordzhonikidze, Leningrad	6 Nov 33	1 Aug 34	4 Aug 35
Shch-309 (ex-Delfin)	#112 Factory, Krasnoe Sormovo, Gorky	6 Nov 33	10 Apr 35	20 Aug 36
Shch-310 (ex-Belukha)	#112 Factory, Krasnoe Sormovo, Gorky	6 Nov 33	10 Apr 35	20 Aug 36
Shch-311 (ex-Kumzha)	#112 Factory, Krasnoe Sormovo, Gorky	6 Nov 33	10 Apr 35	21 Aug 36

Characteristics: 593/705.7 tons, 58.8 oa x 6.2 x 4m, 12.3/8.5 knots, 5250nm at 8 knots/104nm at 2.55 knots, two 45mm/46, two 7.62mm Maxim MGs, four bow + two stern 533mm torpedo tubes, ten torpedoes, 40 men

The results of trials with the previous "Shch" series came in time to facilitate changes. Improved hydrodynamics gave a half-knot boost in speed. Range, quietness, and bulkhead strength increased. Torpedo storage and handling became much more practical.

"M" class, Series VI

Ship	Builder	Laid Down	Launched	Completed
M-1	Marti SY, Nikolayev	3 Oct 32	8 Apr 33	26 Apr 34
M-2	61 Kommunar Yard, Nikolayev	3 Oct 32	8 Apr 33	28 Apr 34
M-3	Marti SY, Nikolayev	2 Oct 32	8 Jun 33	22 May 34

The Series V-bis-2 had a T-shaped antenna spreader and a smooth edge on the fairwater.

Shch-311 *returns from a training sortie to Tallin in May 1941.*

M-4	61 Kommunar Yard, Nikolayev	1 Apr 33	18 Nov 33	2 Jun 34
M-5	61 Kommunar Yard, Nikolayev	1933	29 Oct 33	6 Jun 34
M-6	61 Kommunar Yard, Nikolayev	1932	24 Apr 33	13 Jun 34
M-7	61 Kommunar Yard, Nikolayev	19 Apr 33	5 Aug 33	6 Jul 34
M-8	Marti SY, Nikolayev	31 Oct 32	12 Aug 33	5 Jul 34
M-9	Marti SY, Nikolayev	10 Jan 33	27 Sep 33	5 Jul 34
M-10	61 Kommunar Yard, Nikolayev	1933	24 Aug 33	5 Jul 34
M-11	Marti SY, Nikolayev	16 May 33	29 Nov 33	5 Jul 34
M-12	Marti SY, Nikolayev	26 May 33	2 Dec 33	27 Jul 34
M-13	Marti SY, Nikolayev	7 Jun 33	21 Dec 33	14 Jul 34
M-14	61 Kommunar Yard, Nikolayev	1933	26 Dec 33	10 Jul 34
M-15	61 Kommunar Yard, Nikolayev	1933	26 Dec 33	14 Jul 34
M-16	Marti SY, Nikolayev	5 Aug 33	28 Dec 33	22 Jul 34
M-17	Marti SY, Nikolayev	16 Jul 33	27 Dec 33	21 Jul 34
M-18	Marti SY, Nikolayev	18 Jul 33	24 Dec 33	22 Jul 34
M-19	Marti SY, Nikolayev	20 Jul 33	14 May 34	29 Aug 34
M-20	Marti SY, Nikolayev	25 Aug 33	17 Mar 34	23 Sep 34
M-21	Marti SY, Nikolayev	17 Sep 33	20 Mar 34	23 Sep 34
M-22	Marti SY, Nikolayev	6 Oct 33	15 May 34	10 Oct 34
M-23	61 Kommunar Yard, Nikolayev	1933	16 May 34	10 Oct 34
M-24	Marti SY, Nikolayev	21 Oct 33	1 Jun 34	5 Dec 34
M-25	Marti SY, Nikolayev	1933	16 Jun 34	5 Dec 34
M-26	61 Kommunar Yard, Nikolayev	1933	14 Apr 34	5 Dec 34
M-27	Marti SY, Nikolayev	14 Jun 33	23 Jul 34	31 Dec 34
M-28	Marti SY, Nikolayev	12 Jul 33	21 Jun 34	16 Jul 35
M-51	Marti SY, Nikolayev	17 Nov 32	22 May 33	9 Sep 34
M-52	Marti SY, Nikolayev	15 Aug 33	31 Dec 33	9 Sep 34

Characteristics: 157/197 tons, 36.9 oa x 3.13 x 2.58m, 11.1 knots/6.4 knots, 690nm at 8.6 knots/48nm at 2 knots, one 45mm/46, two bow 533mm torpedo tubes, two torpedoes, 19 men

A Series VI boat in the Pacific Fleet. These boats proved so inferior that all went into reserve before World War II.

M-26 in Vladivostok, showing the distinctive step-down in the hull abaft the fairwater. The torpedoes were "muzzle loaders" inserted tail-first into the tubes before the boat left base.

The driving force behind the "M" class (*malodki* = *maliye lodki* = small boats) was the concept of a coast defense unit transportable by rail in complete condition – no need for breakdown into sections. This would make for strategic flexibility, but in the end, the boats rarely switched theaters.

Design work started with the tsarist *Minoga* of 1909, a prototype that in fact failed to sire any production boats. Though it lacked watertight bulkheads (coming from the same designer as *Bars*), it boasted some advanced features for its time and survived up to 1925. The Series VI boats included bulkheads but continued the *Minoga* concept of an unpretentious, cheap submarine. Prefabricated sections could be built at an inland factory (the Ural Machine Works in Sverdlovsk) without interfering with construction of larger boats in the main yards.

Unfortunately, the humble specifications remained elusive. The first unit to run trials handled poorly and achieved a dive time of 80 seconds, terrible for such a small design. It managed a submerged speed of 5 knots; tinkering to subsequent boats helped them do slightly better. Propulsion depended on a single diesel engine and a single electric motor.

With as many wrinkles as possible ironed out of the Series VI units, what remained was a class with minimal range, tortoise speed, meager habitability, and two torpedoes. Yet the allure of cheap subs prompted further development.

"M" class, Series VI-bis

Ship	Builder	Laid Down	Launched	Completed
M-43 (ex-*M-82*)	Sudomekh, Leningrad	2 Feb 34	10 Jun 35	6 Nov 35
M-44 (ex-*M-84*)	Sudomekh, Leningrad	10 Mar 34	15 Jul 35	27 Nov 35
M-45 (ex-*M-77*, ex-*M-85*)	Marti Yard, Nikolayev	29 May 35	29 Apr 35	4 Nov 35
M-46 (ex-*M-78*, ex-*M-86*)	Marti Yard, Nikolayev	29 Aug 34	10 Jun 35	4 Nov 35
M-47 (ex-*M-53*)	Marti Yard, Nikolayev	10 Feb 34	23 Dec 34	11 Jun 35
M-48 (ex-*M-56*)	61 Kommunar Yard, Nikolayev	25 Mar 35	20 Nov 35	19 Oct 36
M-54	61 Kommunar Yard, Nikolayev	20 Dec 34	15 Sep 35	14 Oct 36
M-55	61 Kommunar Yard, Nikolayev	25 Mar 35	20 Nov 35	17 Oct 36
M-71	Marti Yard, Nikolayev	10 Mar 34	31 Dec 34	13 Sep 35
M-72	Marti Yard, Nikolayev	10 Mar 34	23 Dec 34	13 Sep 35
M-73	Marti Yard, Nikolayev	10 Mar 34	5 Jan 35	13 Sep 35
M-74	Marti Yard, Nikolayev	10 Mar 34	31 Dec 34	13 Sep 35

M-75	Marti Yard, Nikolayev	10 Mar 34	5 Feb 35	13 Sep 35
M-76	Marti Yard, Nikolayev	10 Mar 34	8 Feb 35	13 Sep 35
M-77	Sudomekh, Leningrad	10 Mar 34	21 Mar 35	25 Jun 36
M-78	Sudomekh, Leningrad	20 Mar 34	21 Mar 35	25 Jun 36
M-79	Marti Yard, Nikolayev	25 Aug 34	15 Sep 35	10 Oct 36
M-80	Marti Yard, Nikolayev	25 Aug 34	15 Sep 35	22 Jul 36
M-81	Sudomekh, Leningrad	25 Aug 34	15 Sep 35	22 Jul 36
M-83	Sudomekh, Leningrad	10 Feb 34	1 Jun 35	8 Nov 35

Characteristics: 161/201 tons, 37.8 oa x 3.11 x 2.58m, 13.2 knots/7.2 knots, 1065nm at 10 knots/55nm at 2.5 knots, one 45mm/46, two bow 533mm torpedo tubes, two torpedoes, 19 men

Anticipating many of the Series VI problems, designers started work on corrections even before the boats were built. Series VI-bis had an improved hull form, a new screw design, a rapid-diving tank, and other advances. Yet few of these boats were combat-ready at the start of the war. In reality, though an improvement, the class represented a bluff more than a battle-worthy weapon.

Unlike the Series VI, Series VI-bis had a trapezoidal fairwater and no step in the hull.

Above: *Details of M-55's fairwater, Black Sea 1943. All "M" series carried a single 45mm gun.*

Below: *The Series VI-bis made an early attempt at the streamlined fairwater that would become a trademark of Soviet subs during the Cold War.*

"S" class (originally "N" class), Series IX

Ship	Builder	Laid Down	Launched	Completed
S-1 (ex-N-1)	Ordzhonikidze, Leningrad	25 Dec 34	8 Aug 35	11 Sep 36
S-2 (ex-N-2)	Ordzhonikidze, Leningrad	31 Dec 34	21 Dec 35	11 Sep 36
S-3 (ex-N-3)	Ordzhonikidze, Leningrad	25 Apr 35	30 Apr 36	8 Jul 38

Characteristics: 840/1068.7 tons, 77.75 oa x 6.4 x 4.04m, 19.5/9 knots, 9860nm at 10 knots/148nm at 3 knots, one 100mm/51, one 45mm/46, four bow + two stern 533mm torpedo tubes, twelve torpedoes, 45 men

The Versailles Treaty outlawed submarines of all sorts in Germany, which started German specialists hunting for a way to continue their work. The result was Ingenieurskantoor voor Scheepsbouw (IvS), a ship design company "located" in the Netherlands but in fact thoroughly German. In 1930, work began in Spain on an IvS submarine derived from the German UG design of 1917-18. Planned for the Spanish navy as *E-1*, the boat instead wound up as the Turkish *Gür*, while the design continued to develop into the German Type IA U-boat.

A Soviet party had ventured to Spain to watch *E-1*'s trials, and in 1933, IvS made arrangements to share the plans. The Germans proved less pliant than the Italians, but an agreement was reached. Soviet designers traveled to Germany to help with alterations, including a bigger pair of diesels and a 100mm deck gun, and the design (known variously as Project E-II and Project

224 II) was completed in 1934. German-supplied materiel sped construction of the first two units, but *S-3* fell behind schedule with slow delivery of Soviet diesels and other parts.

German expertise showed in the quietness of the design and in hull details – the same horsepower as in the "P" class yielded a higher submerged speed. The partnership benefited both parties: design experience helped German development toward the Type VII submarine, and the "S" classes certainly ranked among the best Soviet wartime boats.

Series IX started into service with N-numbers but changed in 1937 (S = *Srednaya*, medium).

Above: S-1 *as reconfigured with the deck gun in an open position and a built-up fairwater. Note the salvage ship* Kommuna *in the background.*

Right: *Winter comes to visit S-1. The crenelated design of the fairwater assisted drainage, but later series did not repeat it.*

Opposite: *This grainy photo of a Series IX boat shows the enclosure over the 100mm gun, an unsuccessful feature that was removed prewar.*

"S" class, Series IX-bis

Ship	Builder	Laid Down	Launched	Completed
S-4 (ex-N-4)	Ordzhonikidze, Leningrad	3 Jan 36	17 Sep 36	30 Oct 39
S-5 (ex-N-5)	Ordzhonikidze, Leningrad	28 Dec 35	16 May 36	30 Oct 39
S-6 (ex-N-6)	Ordzhonikidze, Leningrad	28 Nov 35	31 Mar 38	30 Oct 39
S-7 (ex-N-7)	Krasnoye Sormovo, Gorkiy	14 Dec 36	5 Apr 37	30 Jun 40
S-8 (ex-N-8)	Krasnoye Sormovo, Gorkiy	14 Dec 36	5 Apr 37	30 Jun 40
S-9 (ex-N-9)	Krasnoye Sormovo, Gorkiy	20 Jun 36	20 Apr 38	30 Oct 40
S-10 (ex-N-10)	Krasnoye Sormovo, Gorkiy	10 Jun 37	20 Apr 38	25 Dec 40
S-11	Krasnoye Sormovo, Gorkiy	20 Oct 37	20 Apr 38	27 Jun 41
S-12	Krasnoye Sormovo, Gorkiy	20 Oct 37	20 Apr 38	24 Jul 41
S-13	Krasnoye Sormovo, Gorkiy	19 Oct 38	25 Apr 40	31 Jul 41
S-14 Geroicheskii Sevastopol	Krasnoye Sormovo, Gorkiy	31 Oct 38	25 Apr 40	21 Apr 42
S-15 Kolkhoznitsa	Krasnoye Sormovo, Gorkiy	10 Aug 39	24 Apr 40	16 Dec 42
S-16 Geroi Sovetskogo Soyuza Nurseitov	Krasnoye Sormovo, Gorkiy	10 Aug 39	24 Apr 40	20 Feb 43
S-17 Sovetskaya Svanetiya	Krasnoye Sormovo, Gorkiy	10 Aug 39	24 Apr 40	20 Apr 45
S-18	Krasnoye Sormovo, Gorkiy	10 Aug 39	24 Apr 40	20 Jun 45
S-19	Sudomekh, Leningrad	30 Nov 39	14 Mar 41	21 Feb 44
S-20	Sudomekh, Leningrad	30 Nov 39	14 Mar 41	19 Feb 45
S-21	Sudomekh, Leningrad	31 Dec 39	25 Apr 41	29 Mar 46
S-22	Krasnoye Sormovo, Gorkiy	25 Jun 40	2 May 41	25 May 46
S-23	Krasnoye Sormovo, Gorkiy	25 Jun 40	2 May 41	26 Jul 47
S-24	Krasnoye Sormovo, Gorkiy	25 Jun 40	2 May 41	18 Dec 47
S-25	Krasnoye Sormovo, Gorkiy	25 Jun 40	2 May 41	29 Mar 48
S-26	Krasnoye Sormovo, Gorkiy	25 Jun 40	2 May 41	21 Dec 48
S-27	Krasnoye Sormovo, Gorkiy	31 Dec 40	—	—
S-28	Krasnoye Sormovo, Gorkiy	Mar 1941	—	—

S-29	Krasnoye Sormovo, Gorkiy	Mar 1941	—	—
S-30	Krasnoye Sormovo, Gorkiy	Mar 1941	—	—
S-31	Marti Yard, Nikolayev	5 Oct 37	22 Feb 39	19 Jun 40
S-32	Marti Yard, Nikolayev	15 Oct 37	27 Apr 39	19 Jun 40
S-33	Marti Yard, Nikolayev	16 Nov 37	30 May 39	18 Nov 40
S-34	Marti Yard, Nikolayev	29 Nov 37	31 Sep 39	29 Mar 41
S-35	Marti Yard, Nikolayev	23 Feb 40	17 Jul 41	6 Feb 48
S-36	Marti Yard, Nikolayev	23 Feb 40	—	—
S-37	Marti Yard, Nikolayev	27 Nov 40	—	—
S-38	Marti Yard, Nikolayev	22 Feb 41	—	—
S-39	Krasnoye Sormovo, Gorkiy	—	—	—
S-40	Krasnoye Sormovo, Gorkiy	—	—	—
S-41	Krasnoye Sormovo, Gorkiy	—	—	—
S-42	Krasnoye Sormovo, Gorkiy	—	—	—
S-43	Krasnoye Sormovo, Gorkiy	—	—	—
S-44	Krasnoye Sormovo, Gorkiy	—	—	—
S-45	Sudomekh, Leningrad	Dec 1940	—	—
S-46	Sudomekh, Leningrad	Dec 1940	—	—
S-51	Ordzhonikidze, Leningrad	24 Mar 37	30 Aug 40	30 Nov 41
S-52	Ordzhonikidze, Leningrad	29 Apr 37	30 Aug 40	9 Jun 43
S-53	Ordzhonikidze, Leningrad	28 Sep 38	30 Oct 41	30 Dec 43
S-54	Marti Yard, Leningrad	24 Nov 36	4 Nov 38	31 Dec 40
S-55	Marti Yard, Leningrad	24 Nov 36	27 Nov 39	25 Jul 41
S-56	Marti Yard, Leningrad	24 Nov 36	25 Dec 39	20 Oct 41
S-101	Krasnoye Sormovo, Gorkiy	20 Jun 37	20 Apr 38	15 Dec 40
S-102	Krasnoye Sormovo, Gorkiy	20 Jun 37	20 Apr 38	15 Dec 40
S-103	Krasnoye Sormovo, Gorkiy	13 Nov 38	25 Apr 39	30 Jun 42
S-104	Krasnoye Sormovo, Gorkiy	13 Nov 38	25 Apr 39	22 Sep 42

Characteristics: 856/1090 tons, 77.75 oa x 6.43 x 4.04m, 19.45/8.7 knots, 9500nm at 9.6 knots/135nm at 3 knots, one 100mm/51, one 45mm/46, four bow + two stern 533mm torpedo tubes, twelve torpedoes, 45 men

A good look at S-9's net cutter. In general, early units had open-topped fairwaters while later ones had the forward part covered.

S-32 *returns to her Black Sea home port. The forward portion of the fairwater is covered.*

During and after the war, several "S" boats, including S-25 of the Northern Fleet, had a baffle installed halfway up the fairwater to reduce wave impacts.

The Series IX-bis adapted the German project to the realities of Soviet mass production, including the switch from German MAN to Soviet 1D diesels. A trimmed displacement helped prolong the time a boat could maintain its 19.5-knot maximum speed. Production got started with forty-two keels laid, and fourteen boats entered service before the war. The attempt to preserve production from wartime disruption prompted a simplification of the design, sometimes called the Series IX-bis-2. Fifteen such boats were completed during the war, and nine soon afterward. Several units went in sections for assembly at Vladivostok or Astrakhan.

One further batch of the "S" type, Series XVI, got underway, but no units reached completion in wartime.

"Shch" class, Series X

Ship	Builder	Laid Down	Launched	Completed
Shch-126	#194 Factory Marti, Leningrad	23 Jul 34	20 Apr 35	17 Oct 36

Shch-127	#194 Factory Marti, Leningrad	23 Jul 34	13 Jun 35	17 Oct 36
Shch-128	#189 Factory Ordzhonikidze, Leningrad	7 Aug 34	9 Jun 35	31 Oct 36
Shch-129	#194 Factory Marti, Leningrad	31 Dec 34	10 Oct 35	31 Oct 36
Shch-130	#189 Factory Ordzhonikidze, Leningrad	7 Aug 34	8 Aug 35	11 Dec 36
Shch-131	#194 Factory Marti, Leningrad	23 Jul 34	4 Jul 35	11 Dec 36
Shch-132	#194 Factory Marti, Leningrad	31 Dec 34	4 Jul 35	11 Dec 36
Shch-133	#189 Factory Ordzhonikidze, Leningrad	7 Aug 34	4 Jul 35	19 Nov 36
Shch-134	#194 Factory Marti, Leningrad	23 Jul 34	4 Sep 35	27 Dec 36
Shch-208	#200 Factory 61 Kommuna, Nikolayev	18 May 34	7 Oct 35	16 Jan 37
Shch-209	#200 Factory 61 Kommuna, Nikolayev	25 May 34	2 Mar 36	31 Dec 36
Shch-210	#200 Factory 61 Kommuna, Nikolayev	3 Jun 34	13 Mar 36	31 Dec 36
Shch-211	#200 Factory 61 Kommuna, Nikolayev	3 Sep 34	3 Sep 36	5 May 38
Shch-212	#200 Factory 61 Kommuna, Nikolayev	18 Nov 34	29 Dec 36	31 Oct 38
Shch-213	#200 Factory 61 Kommuna, Nikolayev	4 Dec 34	13 Apr 37	31 Oct 38
Shch-214	#200 Factory 61 Kommuna, Nikolayev	13 Jul 35	23 Apr 37	4 Mar 39
Shch-215	#200 Factory 61 Kommuna, Nikolayev	27 Mar 35	11 Jan 37	21 Apr 39
Shch-317	#194 Factory Marti, Leningrad	23 Jul 34	24 Sep 35	29 Sep 36
Shch-318	#194 Factory Marti, Leningrad	23 Jul 34	11 Aug 35	12 Aug 36
Shch-319	#194 Factory Marti, Leningrad	31 Dec 34	15 Feb 36	29 Nov 36
Shch-320	#194 Factory Marti, Leningrad	31 Dec 34	12 Feb 35	29 Nov 36
Shch-322	#112 Factory Krasnoe Sormovo, Gorky	31 Dec 34	10 Apr 35	3 Nov 36
Shch-323	#112 Factory Krasnoe Sormovo, Gorky	31 Dec 34	10 Apr 35	3 Nov 36

Shch-324	#112 Factory Krasnoe Sormovo, Gorky	31 Dec 34	10 Apr 35	31 Oct 36
Shch-401 (ex-*Shch-313*)	#189 Factory Ordzhonikidze, Leningrad	1 Dec 34	28 Jun 35	17 Jul 36
Shch-402 (ex-*Shch-314*)	#189 Factory Ordzhonikidze, Leningrad	4 Dec 34	28 Jun 35	23 Sep 36
Shch-403 (ex-*Shch-315*)	#189 Factory Ordzhonikidze, Leningrad	25 Dec 34	31 Dec 35	26 Sep 36
Shch-404 (ex-*Shch-316*)	#189 Factory Ordzhonikidze, Leningrad	25 Dec 34	27 Dec 35	26 Sep 36
Shch-421 (ex-*Shch-313*)	#112 Factory Krasnoe Sormovo, Gorky	20 Nov 34	12 May 35	5 Dec 37
Shch-422 (ex-*Shch-314*)	#112 Factory Krasnoe Sormovo, Gorky	15 Dec 34	12 Apr 35	4 Dec 37
Shch-139 (ex-*Shch-423*, ex-*Shch-315*)	#112 Factory Krasnoe Sormovo, Gorky	17 Dec 34	27 Apr 35	5 Dec 37
Shch-424 (ex-*Shch-321*, ex-*Shch-312*)	#189 Factory Ordzhonikidze, Leningrad	17 Dec 34	27 Apr 35	17 Jul 36

Characteristics: 584/707.8 tons, 58.75 oa x 6.2 x 3.96m, 14.1/8.5 knots, 4500nm at 8.5 knots/100nm at 2.5 knots, two 45mm/46, four bow + two stern 533mm torpedo tubes, ten torpedoes, 40 men

Shch-212 *leaves Poti on a combat sortie in 1942, passing the battleship* Parizhskaya Kommuna *to one side and the barrels of a Lend-Lease pom-pom to the other. Note the "Som" net cutter installed in the sub's bow.*

This close-up shows the raised 45mm gun platform with fixed sides and the complex periscope and mast shears. Streamlining of the fairwater failed to boost the submerged speed but made the bridge wetter. This is possibly Shch-402.

144

Shch-215 *showing the 12.7mm DShK heavy machine gun and the 25mm 84-K AA cannon, a rare gun system of which fewer than 300 were made. This was probably a local modification as no other boats were thus converted. The inadequacy of the 45mm gun against aircraft prodded many captains to replace it with any available substitute.*

These boats differed little from their predecessors. A streamlined fairwater attempted to improve underwater speed, and a new system for blowing ballast tanks cut two thirds from the 9- to 10-minute emergency surfacing time.

"Shch" class, Series X-bis

Ship	Builder	Laid Down	Launched	Completed
Shch-135	#194 Factory Marti, Leningrad	26 Aug 38	21 Apr 40	1 Sep 41
Shch-136	#194 Factory Marti, Leningrad	26 Aug 38	27 Apr 40	5 Sep 41
Shch-137	#194 Factory Marti, Leningrad	31 Aug 38	22 Jul 40	18 Nov 41
Shch-138	#194 Factory Marti, Leningrad	28 Oct 38	22 Jul 40	30 Dec 41
Shch-216	#200 Factory 61 Kommuna, Nikolayev	23 Jul 38	30 May 40	17 Aug 41
Shch-405	#194 Factory Marti, Leningrad	31 Dec 38	16 Dec 39	7 Jun 41
Shch-406	#194 Factory Marti, Leningrad	31 Dec 38	17 Dec 39	7 Jun 41
Shch-407	#194 Factory Marti, Leningrad	23 Apr 39	4 Jun 40	10 Sep 41
Shch-408	#194 Factory Marti, Leningrad	23 Apr 39	4 Jun 40	10 Sep 41
Shch-409	Murmansk SY, Murmansk	15 Sep 40?	—	—

Shch-216, the only Series X-bis submarine to serve in the Black Sea. Series X-bis differed from Series X in having a drier fairwater (higher and unstreamlined); lowering the forward gun to the deck made a point of distinction from the Series V-bis and V-bis-2.

Shch-410	Murmansk SY, Murmansk	15 Sep 40?	—	—
Shch-411	#194 Factory Marti, Leningrad	29 Jun 39	31 May 41	21 Jul 45
Shch-412	#194 Factory Marti, Leningrad	29 Jun 39	31 May 41	15 Aug 45
Shch-413	#194 Factory Marti, Leningrad	28 Jun 41	—	—
Shch-414	#194 Factory Marti, Leningrad	28 Jun 41	—	—

Characteristics: 590/705 tons normal, 58.75 oa x 6.4 x 4m, 14.4/8.5 knots, 4500nm at 8.5 knots/100nm at 2.8 knots, two 45mm/46, four bow + two stern 533mm torpedo tubes, ten torpedoes, 40 men

The "S" class had established itself as the standard medium submarine, but production delays caused continuation of the "Shch" type with minor improvements. The Series X-bis reverted from the unsuccessful streamlined fairwater of the Series X.

"L" class, Series XI

Ship	Builder	Laid Down	Launched	Completed
L-7 (ex-*Voroshilovets*)	Ordzhonikidze, Leningrad	10 Apr 33	15 May 35	10 Dec 36
L-8 (ex-*Dzerzhinets*)	Ordzhonikidze, Leningrad	10 Apr 33	10 Sep 35	29 Dec 36

Series XI boats had T-shaped antenna spreaders (unlike the Series III's inverted-V) but no stern torpedo tubes (as the Series XIII did).

The 100mm gun of the "L" class.

L-9 (ex-*Kirovets*)	Ordzhonikidze, Leningrad	1 Jun 34	25 Aug 35	10 Dec 36
L-10 (ex-*Menzhinets*)	Marti Yard, Nikolayev	10 Jun 34	18 Dec 36	17 Dec 37
L-11	Marti Yard, Nikolayev	10 Jun 34	4 Dec 36	6 Nov 38
L-12	Marti Yard, Nikolayev	10 Jun 34	7 Nov 36	9 Dec 38

Characteristics: 1040/1340 tons, 79.9 oa x 7 x 3.96 m, 14.5 knots/8.5 knots, 7500nm at 10 knots/135nm at 2.5 knots, one 100mm/51, one 45mm/46, six bow 533mm torpedo tubes, sixteen torpedoes, 20 mines, 55 men

The Series XI, a straightforward improvement of the first "L" class, was most notable as the first series prefabricated in European yards and shipped east for assembly in the Far East. Final work took place at Dalzavod in Vladivostok or at the Amurski Shipyard in Komsomol'skna-Amure.

"M" class, Series XII

Ship	Builder	Laid Down	Launched	Completed
M-30	Krasnoye Sormovo, Gorkiy	20 Jan 38	5 Sep 39	31 Aug 40
M-31	Krasnoye Sormovo, Gorkiy	31 Aug 38	25 Feb 40	7 Nov 40
M-32	Krasnoye Sormovo, Gorkiy	31 Aug 38	26 Feb 40	7 Nov 40
M-33	Krasnoye Sormovo, Gorkiy	31 Aug 38	23 Jun 40	19 Jan 41
M-34	Krasnoye Sormovo, Gorkiy	22 Feb 39	23 Jun 40	11 Jan 41
M-35	Krasnoye Sormovo, Gorkiy	22 Feb 39	20 Aug 40	22 Feb 41
M-36	Krasnoye Sormovo, Gorkiy	22 Feb 39	20 Aug 40	29 Apr 41
M-49 (ex-M-57)	Krasnoye Sormovo, Gorkiy	26 Jul 37	25 Jan 39	3 Aug 39
M-58	Krasnoye Sormovo, Gorkiy	25 Oct 37	28 Apr 39	10 Oct 39
M-59	Krasnoye Sormovo, Gorkiy	25 Oct 37	13 Jun 39	19 Jun 40
M-60	Krasnoye Sormovo, Gorkiy	25 Oct 37	28 Aug 39	19 Jun 40
M-62 (ex-M-59)	Krasnoye Sormovo, Gorkiy	20 Jan 38	5 Oct 39	31 Aug 40
M-63 (ex-M-60)	Krasnoye Sormovo, Gorkiy	20 Jan 38	5 Oct 39	31 Jul 40
M-90	Sudomekh, Leningrad	27 Jun 36	28 Nov 37	25 Jun 38
M-94	Sudomekh, Leningrad	25 Dec 38	11 Sep 39	12 Dec 39
M-95	Sudomekh, Leningrad	25 Dec 38	11 Sep 39	12 Dec 39

M-96	Krasnoye Sormovo, Gorkiy	26 Jul 37	20 Jul 38	12 Dec 39
M-97	Krasnoye Sormovo, Gorkiy	26 Jul 37	20 Jul 38	12 Nov 39
M-98	Sudomekh, Leningrad	22 Jun 39	15 Apr 40	1 Aug 40
M-99	Sudomekh, Leningrad	26 Jun 39	15 Apr 40	23 Jul 40
M-102	Sudomekh, Leningrad	15 May 40	12 Oct 40	29 Dec 40
M-103	Sudomekh, Leningrad	31 May 40	12 Oct 40	29 Dec 40
M-104 Yaroslavskiy Komsomolets	Krasnoye Sormovo, Gorkiy	30 Oct 40	24 Sep 42	24 Feb 43
M-105 Chelyabinskiy Komsomolets	Krasnoye Sormovo, Gorkiy	30 Oct 40	30 Sep 42	17 Mar 43
M-106 Leninskiy Komsomolets	Krasnoye Sormovo, Gorkiy	30 Oct 40	9 Oct 42	28 Apr 43
M-107 Novosibirskiy Komsomolets	Krasnoye Sormovo, Gorkiy	30 Oct 40	6 Dec 42	18 Jun 43
M-108	Krasnoye Sormovo, Gorkiy	30 Oct 40	9 Jan 43	24 Aug 43
M-111	Krasnoye Sormovo, Gorkiy	25 Oct 39	31 Dec 40	5 Jul 41
M-112	Krasnoye Sormovo, Gorkiy	25 Oct 39	31 Dec 40	5 Jul 41
M-113	Krasnoye Sormovo, Gorkiy	25 Oct 39	31 Dec 40	5 Jul 41
M-114	Krasnoye Sormovo, Gorkiy	27 Nov 39	7 May 41	12 Nov 41
M-115	Krasnoye Sormovo, Gorkiy	27 Nov 39	7 May 41	1 Oct 41
M-116	Krasnoye Sormovo, Gorkiy	27 Nov 39	7 May 41	7 Nov 41
M-117	Krasnoye Sormovo, Gorkiy	29 Jan 40	12 Feb 41	8 Nov 41
M-118	Krasnoye Sormovo, Gorkiy	29 Jan 40	12 Feb 41	8 Nov 41
M-119	Krasnoye Sormovo, Gorkiy	28 May 40	26 Jun 41	29 Oct 42
M-120	Krasnoye Sormovo, Gorkiy	28 Jan 40	29 Jun 41	8 Nov 41
M-121	Krasnoye Sormovo, Gorkiy	28 May 40	19 Aug 41	10 Apr 42
M-122	Krasnoye Sormovo, Gorkiy	28 May 40	1 Aug 42	5 Nov 42
M-171 (ex-M-87)	Sudomekh, Leningrad	10 Sep 36	23 Jul 37	11 Dec 37
M-172 (ex-M-88)	Sudomekh, Leningrad	17 Jun 36	23 Jul 37	25 Dec 37

M-173 (ex-M-89)	Sudomekh, Leningrad	27 Jun 36	9 Oct 37	22 Jun 38
M-174 (ex-M-91)	Sudomekh, Leningrad	29 May 37	12 Oct 37	21 Jun 39
M-175 (ex-M-92)	Sudomekh, Leningrad	29 May 37	12 Oct 37	21 Jun 39
M-176 (ex-M-93)	Sudomekh, Leningrad	29 May 37	12 Oct 37	21 Jun 39

Characteristics: 206/258 tons, 44.5 oa x 3.3 x 2.85m, 14.4 knots/7.8 knots, 3380nm at 8.6 knots/108nm at 2.9 knots, one 45mm/46, two bow 533mm torpedo tubes, two torpedoes, 20 men

The 50-ton increase bought a significant improvement over previous "M" classes. Range, submerged and surface, dramatically increased. Speeds became competitive. Dive time shrank to a reasonable 35 seconds. The "M" class had finally become battleworthy, and the boats took an active role in the war.

Forty-five completions made this the most numerous group of Soviet wartime submarines, and some references split the boats into two series, XII and XII-bis. The Soviets diverted two additional hulls for experiments in submerged diesel operation, *M-92* and *M-401*.

The fairwater provided as much room as possible and some shelter.

Opposite: *The Northern Fleet's M-171 before her minelayer conversion. The relatively large fairwater had some streamlining as was fashionable at the time in Soviet designs.*

Below: *A good view of the 45mm 21-K anti-aircraft gun. The number in the star indicates the sub's victory claims.*

The "M" class required a unique torpedo-loading process.

"L" class, Series XIII

Ship	Builder	Laid Down	Launched	Completed
L-13	Ordzhonikidze, Leningrad	25 Apr 35	2 Aug 36	2 Oct 38
L-14	Ordzhonikidze, Leningrad	25 Apr 35	20 Dec 36	10 Oct 38
L-15	Marti Yard, Nikolaev	5 Nov 35	26 Dec 36	6 Nov 38
L-16	Marti Yard, Nikolaev	5 Nov 35	9 Jul 37	9 Dec 38
L-17	Marti Yard, Nikolaev	25 Jan 36	5 Nov 37	5 Jun 39
L-18	Ordzhonikidze, Leningrad	30 Dec 35	12 May 38	10 Oct 39
L-19	Ordzhonikidze, Leningrad	26 Dec 35	25 May 38	4 Nov 39

Characteristics: 1120/1425 tons, 85.3 oa x 7.0 x 4.05m, 15/9 knots submerged, 10,000nm at 10 knots/150nm at 2.7 knots, one 100mm/51, one 45mm/46, one 12.7mm DShK mg, one 7.62mm mg, six bow + two stern 533mm torpedo tubes, eighteen torpedoes, 18 PLT mines, 56 men

The "L" type took a step forward with the Series XIII, gaining a set of stern torpedoes, an increase in depth limits, and an increase in range. Dive time

L-18 shows typical Series XIII features: a long, low fairwater; the prominent periscope shears behind the covered bridge area, rather than at the front as in the Series XI; a raised bow; and T-shaped antenna spreaders.

153

L-17, *Series XIII; the broad bow improved sea-keeping. Note the slightly raised gun platform.*

Opposite: L-21 *of the Baltic Fleet passes the distinctive stern of the "K" class.*

went from 80 to 45 seconds. A cable-drive minelaying system replaced the chain drive for quieter performance, at the cost of one mine per tube. Once again, all the boats shipped east for assembly at Dalzavod, Vladivostok.

"L" class, Series XIII-38 (also known as Series XIII-bis)

Ship	Builder	Laid Down	Launched	Completed
L-20	Ordzhonikidze, Leningrad	10 June 38	14 Apr 40	28 Aug 42
L-21	Ordzhonikidze, Leningrad	l0 Jun 38	17 Jul 40	8 Aug 43
L-22	Ordzhonikidze, Leningrad	4 Dec 38	23 Sep 39	28 Aug 42
L-23	Marti Yard, Nikolayev	17 Oct 38	29 Apr 40	31 Oct 41
L-24	Marti Yard, Nikolayev	20 Oct 38	17 Dec 40	29 Apr 42
L-25	Marti Yard, Nikolayev	23 Oct 38	26 Feb 41	—

Characteristics: 1108/1400 tons, 83.3 oa x 7.0 x 4.05m, 18/9 knots, 10,000nm at 10 knots/150nm at 2.5 knots, one 100mm/51, one 45mm/46, two 7.62mm mg, six bow + two stern 533mm torpedo tubes, twenty torpedoes, 20 PLT mines, 56 men

The Pacific Fleet now boasted twelve of the navy's eighteen submarine minelayers, and the decision was made to build six more for European duty. The new class received 1D diesels and higher surface speed. The cable-drive deployment system regained its two lost mines.

L-22 in 1943. Visually, the Series XIII-38 was nearly indistinguishable from the Series XIII, but Series XIII-38 lacked T-shaped antenna spreaders and had its 100mm gun platform flush with the deck.

Minelayers of the Northern Fleet's 1st Division perform an anti-aircraft drill with the standard 100mm and 45mm guns.

The war disrupted construction. *L-20* and *L-22* were brought successfully to Molotovsk for completion. *L-23* and *L-24* escaped Nikolayev incomplete, but both eventually entered service on the Black Sea. *L-25* was not so lucky, striking a mine while under tow.

"K" class, Series XIV (Project 41)

Ship	Builder	Laid Down	Launched	Completed
K-1	Marti Yard, Leningrad	27 Dec 36	29 Apr 38	26 May 40
K-2	Marti Yard, Leningrad	27 Dec 36	29 Apr 38	26 May 40
K-3	Marti Yard, Leningrad	27 Dec 36	31 Jul 38	19 Dec 40
K-21	Ordzhonikidze, Leningrad	10 Dec 37	16 Aug 39	3 Feb 41
K-22	Ordzhonikidze, Leningrad	5 Jan 38	3 Nov 38	7 Aug 40
K-23	Ordzhonikidze, Leningrad	5 Feb 38	28 Apr 39	25 Oct 40
K-51	Ordzhonikidze, Leningrad	26 Feb 38	30 Jul 39	20 Dec 43
K-52	Ordzhonikidze, Leningrad	26 Feb 38	5 Jul 39	11 Oct 42
K-53	Ordzhonikidze, Leningrad	30 May 38	2 Sep 39	31 Aug 43
K-54	Marti Yard, Leningrad	30 Apr 37	8 Mar 41	—
K-55	Marti Yard, Leningrad	29 Apr 37	7 Feb 41	25 Dec 44
K-56	Marti Yard, Leningrad	17 Oct 37	29 Dec 40	25 Nov 42

Characteristics: 1500/2117 tons, 97.7 oa x 7.4 x 4.04m, 22/10.3 knots, 16,500nm at 9 knots/175nm at 2.9 knots, two 100mm/51, two 45mm/46, two 7.62mm mgs, six bow + two stern + two external aft 533mm torpedo tubes, twenty-four torpedoes, 20 EP-36 mines, 62-65 men

The Soviets had an unpleasant precedent in their first cruiser submarine effort, the "P" class, but the great success of the Series XIV shows how far they had advanced in just a few years. The "K" class performed well on almost every level.

The project germinated shortly after the first peaks at the *E-1* plans, and that input helped the proposed KE-9 plan (KE = Cruising, Squadron) win approval. Originally it was hoped to include a hangar for a seaplane, but the nominated aircraft turned out too flimsy in trials; an improved type implied a larger one, implying a larger hangar and an undue burden on the submarine design.

The "K's" met the challenge of the specified surface speed, perhaps surpassing it on trials. The hull provided good seakeeping and relatively spacious accommodations for long patrols. Diving time was adequate at about 60 seconds.

However, like all warship designs, Series XIV had its weaknesses. The mine tubes served also for ballast and fuel storage, and mining operations suffered for the lack of specialization; the "K's" ceased to carry mines in 1944. Hull plating would have benefited from greater thickness. In general, Soviet designs lagged behind foreign standards in diving depth and quietness. In 1944, American inspections of *K-21* and *K-52* revealed a design deemed workmanlike but technically inferior.

K-21 achieved special notoriety for managing an attack on the German battleship *Tirpitz* as she sortied from Norway in 1942. Despite the claim of a torpedo hit, the Germans passed through the attack without ever noticing, but interception of *K-21*'s radio report helped convince the Germans to abort their mission.

An improved class, twenty fully-welded boats of the "KU" type, would have had longer endurance and a speed of 24 knots. However, the project never got underway.

Northern Fleet boat K-21 returns from a combat sortie on 9 July 1942. The "K" class was the largest, best-armed, and longest-ranged design in Soviet service.

Later units had a raised and bulged bow for improved sea-keeping. The "K's" were intended for the Northern and Pacific Fleets, but the war trapped K-53 and K-56 and three others in the Baltic where their size was a handicap.

The aft weaponry included two external tubes.

Left: The "K" class carried its 100mm guns in the turret-like mounts.

Below: Details of the 100mm B-24 gun and the turret arrangement. This gun replaced the unsuccessful 102mm B-2 gun in the earlier "D," "L," and "P" classes and served from the start in the "S" and "K" classes.

"M" class, Series XV (Project 96)

Ship	Builder	Laid Down	Launched	Completed
M-200 Mest	Sudomekh, Leningrad	31 Mar 40	17 Jul 41	20 Mar 43
M-201	Sudomekh, Leningrad	31 Mar 40	17 Jul 41	16 Apr 43
M-202 Rybnik Donbasa	Sudomekh, Leningrad	25 May 40	15 Jul 41	19 Jul 44
M-203 Irkutskiy Rybak	Sudomekh, Leningrad	31 Oct 40	7 Jul 41	28 Oct 45
M-204	Sudomekh, Leningrad	31 Oct 40	17 Jul 46	25 Jun 47
M-205	Sudomekh, Leningrad	30 Dec 40	10 Nov 46	22 Jul 47
M-206	Sudomekh, Leningrad	31 Dec 40	26 Apr 47	30 Sep 47
M-207	Sudomekh, Leningrad	—	—	—
M-208	Sudomekh, Leningrad	—	—	—
M-209	Sudomekh, Leningrad	—	—	—
M-210	Sudomekh, Leningrad	—	—	—
M-211	Sudomekh, Leningrad	—	—	—
M-212	Sudomekh, Leningrad	—	—	—
M-213	Sudomekh, Leningrad	—	—	—
M-214	Karsnoye Sormovo, Gorkiy	30 May 41	24 Sep 46	14 Aug 48
M-215	Sudomekh, Leningrad	30 Apr 41	22 Jul 47	31 Oct 47
M-216	Sudomekh, Leningrad	30 Apr 41	26 Jui 47	5 Nov 47
M-217	Sudomekh, Leningrad	30 Apr 41	26 Jul 47	10 Nov 47
M-218	Sudomekh, Leningrad	30 Apr 41	10 Sep 47	10 Nov 47
M-219	Karsnoye Sormovo, Gorkiy	30 Apr 41	—	—
M-220	Sudomekh, Leningrad	—	—	—
M-221	Sudomekh, Leningrad	—	—	—
M-222	Sudomekh, Leningrad	—	—	—
M-223	Sudomekh, Leningrad	—	—	—
M-224	Sudomekh, Leningrad	—	—	—
M-225	Sudomekh, Leningrad	—	—	—

M-226	Sudomekh, Leningrad	—	—	—
M-227	Sudomekh, Leningrad	—	—	—
M-228	Sudomekh, Leningrad	—	—	—
M-229	Sudomekh, Leningrad	—	—	—
M-230	Sudomekh, Leningrad	—	—	—
M-231	Sudomekh, Leningrad	—	—	—
M-232	Sudomekh, Leningrad	—	—	—
M-233	Sudomekh, Leningrad	—	—	—
M-234	Karsnoye Sormovo, Gorkiy	20 Jun 41	25 Apr 48	31 Oct 48
M-235	Karsnoye Sormovo, Gorkiy	20 Jun 41	25 Apr 48	25 Aug 48
M-236	Karsnoye Sormovo, Gorkiy	19 Feb 47	19 Jun 48	1948
M-237	Karsnoye Sormovo, Gorkiy	15 Mar 47	27 Jul 48	29 Nov 48
M-238	Karsnoye Sormovo, Gorkiy	25 Apr 47	21 Aug 48	7 Dec 48
M-239	Sudomekh, Leningrad	7 Jul 47	2 Oct 48	14 Jul 49
M-240	Sudomekh, Leningrad	27 Aug 48	22 Nov 48	30 Jul 49
M-241	Sudomekh, Leningrad	31 Aug 48	30 Dec 48	30 Jul 49
M-242	Sudomekh, Leningrad	30 Sep 48	30 Mar 49	30 Jul 49
M-243	Sudomekh, Leningrad	31 Oct 48	30 Apr 49	31 Aug 49
M-244	Sudomekh, Leningrad	24 Nov 48	01 Jun 49	1 Oct 49
M-245	Sudomekh, Leningrad	30 Nov 48	30 Jun 49	31 Oct 49
M-246	Sudomekh, Leningrad	25 Jan 49	24 Jul 49	16 Nov 49
M-247	Sudomekh, Leningrad	14 Feb 49	31 Aug 49	22 Nov 49
M-248	Sudomekh, Leningrad	24 Feb 49	29 Sep 49	23 Nov 49
M-249	Sudomekh, Leningrad	25 Apr 49	30 Oct 49	31 Dec 49
M-250	Sudomekh, Leningrad	28 Jun 49	28 Nov 49	2 Jun 50
M-251	Sudomekh, Leningrad	23 Sep 49	22 Dec 49	25 Jun 50
M-252	Sudomekh, Leningrad	22 Oct 49	25 Jun 50	10 Jul 50
M-253	Sudomekh, Leningrad	9 Nov 49	30 Mar 50	29 Jul 50
M-270	Sudomekh, Leningrad	23 Dec 49	24 Apr 50	29 Jul 50

M-271	Sudomekh, Leningrad	31 Jan 50	30 Apr 50	28 Aug 50
M-272	Sudomekh, Leningrad	25 Feb 50	13 Jun 50	11 Sep 50
M-273	Sudomekh, Leningrad	18 Mar 50	20 Jul 50	28 Sep 50
M-274	Sudomekh, Leningrad	29 Apr 50	18 Sep 50	31 Oct 50
M-275	Sudomekh, Leningrad	25 May 50	23 Sep 50	15 Nov 50
M-276	Sudomekh, Leningrad	28 Jun 50	17 Oct 50	25 Dec 50
M-277	Sudomekh, Leningrad	31 Jul 50	1950-51	24 May 51
M-278	Sudomekh, Leningrad	31 Aug 50	19 Jan 51	28 May 51
M-279	Sudomekh, Leningrad	12 Oct 50	10 Feb 51	9 Jun 51
M-280	Sudomekh, Leningrad	20 Dec 50	14 Apr 51	21 Jul 51
M-281	Sudomekh, Leningrad	4 Feb 51	3 Jul 51	23 Aug 51
M-282	Sudomekh, Leningrad	11 Mar 51	12 Jun 51	14 Sep 51
M-283	Sudomekh, Leningrad	2 Apr 51	3 Jul 51	30 Sep 51
M-284	Sudomekh, Leningrad	3 May 51	11 Aug 51	31 Oct 51
M-285	Sudomekh, Leningrad	31 May 51	14 Sep 51	12 Feb 52
M-286	Sudomekh, Leningrad	29 Jun 51	15 Oct 51	25 Jun 52
M-287	Sudomekh, Leningrad	25 Jun 51	15 Nov 51	25 Jun 52
M-288	Sudomekh, Leningrad	24 Aug 51	24 Jan 52	24 Jul 52
M-289	Sudomekh, Leningrad	27 Sep 51	28 Apr 52	27 Aug 52
M-290	Sudomekh, Leningrad	10 Nov 51	1 Jul 52	30 Sep 52
M-291	Sudomekh, Leningrad	28 Dec 51	1 Jul 52	25 Nov 52
M-292	Sudomekh, Leningrad	15 Apr 52	30 Sep 52	12 Jan 53
M-293	Sudomekh, Leningrad	10 Feb 52	02 Oct 52	12 Jan 53
M-294	Sudomekh, Leningrad	29 May 52	22 Oct 52	26 Feb 53

Characteristics: 281/351 tons, 50.5 oa x 4.4 x 2.81m, 15.5 knots/7.9 knots, 4500nm at 8 knots/85nm at 2.9 knots, one 45mm/46, four bow 533mm torpedo tubes, four torpedoes, 32 men

Series XV continued the "M" class improvement. The doubling of the torpedo tubes did not address the lack of reloads or the inability to access and service the weapons during patrol. The power plant expanded, now two diesels and two electric motors, which provided a more realistic range and some redundancy in the case of a machinery casualty.

A Series XV boat shows its profile.

The Series XV had a smaller but taller fairwater with an open bridge, almost German in appearance.

The initial order included twenty-two boats, of which fifteen began building. Only four boats reached completion in time for war service, ten followed after the war, and one hull became a fuel tank. The series got a second life in 1947 with orders for fifty-three more units.

Several incomplete units were evacuated to Astrakhan on the Caspian Sea. Of the four wartime Series XV submarines, two served in the Northern Fleet and two in the Black Sea.

The Russians had purchased submarines overseas during World War I, and the Soviets had salvaged Britain's *L-55* in the 1920s. But the World War II years saw the acquisitions of numerous foreign boats, some through Allied transfer, and others by less amicable means.

Upon gobbling up the Baltic States, the Soviets gained two pairs of subs. Estonia's British-built *Kalev*s proved quite useful in minelaying and in patrol. The Latvian *Ronis* class, small boats built in France, never operated with the Soviets. Sent for refits shortly after their acquisition, they were unable to evacuate Libau before the Germans arrived, and both were scuttled.

Among the ships transferred to the Soviet Union in lieu of Italian war reparations were four modern British subs, one from the "S" class and three from the "U" class. *V-1* (ex-*Sunfish*) fell victim to friendly fire while en route to her new owners. The others – *V-2* (ex-*Unbroken*), *V-3* (ex-*Unison*), and *V-4* (ex-*Ursula*) – survived their stint with the Red fleet and returned to British custody in 1949, replaced in Soviet service by the ex-Italian *Marea* and *Nichelio*.

Romania had a modest submarine force, which ceded to Soviet control. Some of the boats were in poor condition, especially the set of former Italian four-man midget subs. The full-sized boats *TS-1* (ex-*Requinul*) and *TS-2* (ex-*Marsuinul*) were IvS products. The Italian-built *TS-3* (ex-*Delfinul*) had left service two years before the Soviets took her.

The Estonian Lembit *and* Kalev, *showing their unique hull form. Unlike Soviet types with their long horizontal mine tubes inside the hull, they carried vertical tubes in the side sponsons, two mines per tube.*

The details of Kalev's *sizeable fairwater and periscopes.*

The open bridge and the gun behind the fairwater distinguish Spidola *from Soviet submarines.*

Ronis *and* Spidola *while still in Latvian service. Note the low shield around the bridge.*

V-1 *(foreground) with* V-4 *on the day of transfer to Soviet control.*

Rechinul's *German origins are obvious in her appearance. – courtesy of Modelism.*

CHAPTER 5

Other Surface Vessels

The vagaries of Soviet policy never obscured the central purpose of the navy as the army's shield-bearer in defending the homeland from invasion. It was in this role that the navy expended its greatest effort and achieved its greatest success. The gunboats and monitors were often key in providing direct support to army movements.

One of the longest-serving combatants, Krasnoe Znamya *was launched in 1895 as* Khabryy. *She went on to experience multiple modifications and rebuilds. Seen here in the 1920s, she carries five 130mm guns. She had one more rebuild before World War II and didn't retire until 1961.*

Krasny Azerbaidzhan *in wartime. As with the other ex-tsarist gunboats, extensive modernization allowed for a lengthy career. This view shows that the sponsons have been faired over and anti-aircraft guns have been added on the sides of the superstructure.*

Based on self-beaching Azov Sea lighters, the El'pidifor *class began construction in 1917 as landing craft for a Bosporus invasion, but also meant as minecraft, transports, rescue ships, gunboats, etc. Most units entered mercantile service, but four remained with the navy into World War II, including* Krasnaya Abkhaziya, *seen here.*

170

Sverdlov *shows how modernization with a fire-control station atop a large tripod had altered the clean silhouettes of the Amur River monitors. The ships played "musical turrets" with each other; originally mounting two 152mm single turrets and two 120mm twins, by 1941 they all had homogeneous batteries. Some ships traded their 152mm guns for 130mm guns.*

Zheleznyakov *had to share her name with a* Novik-*class destroyer. Her sister-ships all sank in 1941, but she survived with the enhanced anti-aircraft armament seen here in 1945: 37mm cannon mounted aft and a quad Vickers machine gun atop the superstructure.*

The powerful monitors Khasan *and* Sivash *during a Navy Day parade, showing superstructure details with the fire-control station on her tripod mast and the twin 76mm 39-K turrets.*

Moskva, *from a class of auxiliary gunboats that carried various weaponry and some interesting camouflage.*

The fighting around Stalingrad prompted the fitting of 100mm guns aboard the Volga sidewheeler Usyskin *and six sister-ships.*

KL-41, *seen here in 1943, typified the improvised gunboats that served on Soviet rivers and lakes during the war: a tugboat armed with available weaponry (in this case an 85mm army gun and a 37mm naval cannon along with machine guns) to provide fire support and convoy protection.*

The spectrum of designs serving as patrol ships ran from purpose-built fleet units armed with torpedoes down to commandeered fishing vessels armed with whatever weapons presented themselves. These craft did not all serve under the same leadership. The NKVD – the state security force – controlled its own set of vessels, initially outside the naval chain of command. With several entities overseeing forces afloat, it was not unusual for one name to be used for several vessels at the same time.

Above: *The Italian-built* Kirov *was not a cruiser, but an NKVD patrol vessel.*

Left: Smerch *of the* Uragan *class in 1942, wearing an unusual camouflage scheme and canvas for her bridge. The eighteen* Uragans *were the first fleet units built by the Soviets, affording them the first chance to display all the problems with Soviet industry and administration. They nevertheless served actively during the war.*

Project 29 represented the next generation of the patrol ships of the new ocean-going navy, but once again war mangled the program. Of thirty units planned, only fourteen began building, and only Yastreb *(seen here in 1945) commissioned before war's end. Compared to* Uragan, *Project 29 mounted an extra 100mm gun aft, regardless of the crowding.*

EK-2 (ex-Charlottesville), one of the twenty-eight American Tacoma-*class frigates provided under Lend-Lease. They transferred to the Soviet Pacific Fleet in summer 1945 just in time to participate in the attack on Japan. Their Soviet service lasted until 1949.*

Zarya was among the thirty-four trawlers mobilized as patrol ships in the Northern Fleet. The vast expanse of the northern region required a multitude of patrol vessels, and these hardy trawlers came in handy.

The MO-4 class – 219 submarine-chaser units, plus 44 built for the NKVD – formed the mainstay of the Soviet anti-submarine force. Lacking sonar, they had limited value against submarines but proved useful for other roles, such as patrol, convoy escort, and landing of reconnaissance parties. Their semi-automatic 45mm guns put them at disadvantage against German S-Boats armed with fast-firing cannon.

The Soviets participated little in open-sea escort, but they built a number of submarine chasers suitable for a variety of tasks in coastal waters. Soviet anti-submarine technology didn't match the sophistication seen in some major fleets, but the *Artillerist* class did introduce an active sonar.

Sixty-six units of the BMO class addressed most of the problems with the MO-4 design. They carried automatic weapons (a 37mm cannon and six 12.7mm machine guns) and plates of bulletproof armor.

Twenty-three Artillerist-*class submarine-chasers (this one seen postwar) served in wartime, greatly improving on the smaller types. The dual-purpose 85mm gun and two 37mm cannon gave more punch against ships and aircraft, and the Tamir-3 sonar provided a genuine anti-submarine potential.*

The Imperial yacht Shtandart, *completed in 1896, was laid up after the Revolution. In the 1930s, the navy noticed she remained in fine condition and still had many years left in her. She underwent a complete rebuild and emerged in 1936 as* Marti, *a minelayer with a cruiserish look. In fact, the Germans often misidentified her as a cruiser. Armed with four 130mm guns and seven 76mm DP guns and able to carry 416 mines, she had a speed of just 14.5 knots, inadequate for offensive operations.*

Converted minelayers like Okhotsk *were a primary defense for the Pacific Fleet. The Soviets knew they had no hope of matching Japan's powerful navy, so they converted several cargo ships to mine the approaches to harbors in case of war.*

Built in the dozens, the Fugas*-class minesweepers had traditional features like a canvas-covered bridge, a 100mm main gun, and a 45mm anti-aircraft gun, along with an untraditional feature – diesel propulsion. Early units, like* T-401 Tral *seen here leaving Novorossiysk for Sevastopol in 1942, entered service before the diesels had all their bugs worked out.*

Name-ship of Vladimir Polukhin *class. This brawny, turbine-powered design gestated under the "Big Fleet" program which dictated long range and speed to accompany the battle fleet. Of the twenty units begun prewar, two commissioned in wartime, thirteen came postwar modified with diesels, and five became war casualties before completion.*

The Russians established an early expertise in mine warfare and had great success with it in the Russo-Japanese War and World War I. Many designs featured minelaying gear, so dedicated minelayers were few. Minesweepers appeared in great numbers – specialized warships, converted merchant craft, and motor boats.

Among the most flexible and successful units in the Soviet navy were its motor boats. The leadership in the 1920s had an ideological liking for MTBs, and steady effort went into development and production, extending through the war years. Available in large numbers, the MTBs scored successes in the Baltic, the Black Sea, and the Arctic; they served in many capacities, including minelaying and even amphibious landings.

A line of armored MGBs also appeared in large numbers. Many of them mounted tank guns as their main armament along with machine guns, rockets, and a variety of other weapons. It was a simple and practical concept perfectly matched to Soviet needs and capabilities.

BK2 *dated from World War I. Her class continued in service during the Civil War and into World War II when all remaining units were lost in the Dniepr flotilla.*

The Project 1125 BKAs (bronevoy katery = armored cutters) rate among the most important warships in the Soviet navy – small and hardly glamorous, but stoutly armored and armed with one T-28 or T-34 tank turret plus machine guns. They fought in nearly every battle that involved rivers and even participated in taking Berlin. A total of 151 of these boats were built between 1933 and war's end.

A Project S-40 BKA, a diesel version of Project 1125 designed for the Amur River. The production bottleneck for tank diesels limited completions to only seven craft. Many BKAs carried 82mm M-8-M or 132mm M-13-M Katyusha rocket launchers for ground support.

Project 1124 produced ninety-seven completions, large boats armed with two tank turrets. Many received firepower upgrades with mortars, rocket launchers, or even 37mm cannon.

Red forces captured some small British CMBs in 1920, and ensuing design studies emphasized the speed of small boats rather than the sea-keeping of larger craft. Here is Pervenets *of 1927, the first Soviet-built MTB, capable of 56 knots.*

The Soviets built 329 MTBs of the G-5 class between 1933 and 1945, making it the most numerous Soviet combatant class to that date. A G-5 sank the 1500-ton German torpedo boat T-31, the largest warship sunk by Soviet surface forces.

Close-up of the G-5 superstructure. Note the extremely cramped conditions. The G-5 could carry two 533 torpedoes in stern troughs and one or two 12.7mm DShK machine guns. Some also mounted M-8-M 82mm rocket launchers.

Boats of the D-3 class, like TKA-116, could reach only 32 knots but excelled the G-5 boats in almost all other ways. Twice as large as a G-5, a D-3 fired its torpedoes from tubes – much safer and more accurate than dropping them from stern troughs.

The Soviets completed only a handful of TM-200 "Yunga" MTBs during the war, but the design formed the basis of postwar types. They matched the size of American MTBs and neared their capabilities except in speed and range. Armament included three 12.7mm DShK and two 533mm torpedoes as well as radar.

CHAPTER 6

Epilogue

In terms of lives lost, the Soviets paid an astounding price in World War II, and they suffered materiel destruction on a similar scale. One of the casualties prominent in military circles was the fleet's growth campaign which had advanced to the brink of completing its first modern battleships. With the war's end, a new campaign got underway as the Soviets scrambled for a maximum share of the spoils. With their foreign equipment and weaponry, captive ships typically have limited value, often worth more as scrap than as warships. But after four years of rough handling, the admiralty saw any seaworthy hull as a potential reinforcement. For designers, such ships promised a host of lessons which, mixed with the wealth of war experience, would form the basis for construction in the 1950s and beyond. In the meanwhile, war booty provided platforms for training and other mundane necessities in a fleet that would soon challenge for global preeminence.

Ships from Romania and Bulgaria had already been impressed into Soviet service during the final phase of the push into Germany. Finland had the special privilege of a second Soviet defeat in five years; having already ceded some ships at the conclusion of the Winter War, the Finns in 1947 surrendered the only large warship they had remaining, along with some passenger ships and lesser assets.

A German-designed coast defense ship, Viborg *served as Finland's* Väinämöinen *until 1947. With her 10-inch guns, she packed more punch than any other Soviet units short of the battleships. By prize standards, she had a long Soviet career, going into reserve in 1959 and to the breakers in 1966.*

Whittled down from among the world's strongest fleets in 1941, the Japanese Navy had little remaining at war's end. The brief Soviet commitment to fighting Japan in 1945 produced a modest naval harvest: various gunboats and small craft captured during the Manchurian offensive, and nothing larger than a destroyer as reparations. Japanese ships lasted a remarkably short time in Soviet service, most retiring from active duty by 1949.

One of Japan's Improved Type B "sea defense ships." Two of these vessels were among the escorts ceded to the Soviets. —courtesy of Lars Ahlberg.

Fourteen of the seventeen ex-Japanese escorts came from the Types C and D. These two classes, basically identical except for their propulsion machinery, were simplified and reduced from Type B standards to facilitate mass production.

Major units from Japan

> Destroyers: 7
> Escorts: 17
> Gunboats: 4
> Landing Craft: 1
> Minecraft: 3

After six years of waiting, Stalin finally got a share of the surrendered Italian fleet, a total of 45 ships. This included his prized catch, the battleship *Novorossiysk* (ex-*Giulio Cesare*). Though completed in the same year as *Sevastopol*, *Cesare* underwent elaborate reconstruction in the 1930s and emerged greatly superior. Even so, she was a disappointment to the Soviets, who wanted one of Italy's new *Littorio*-class ships. The Western Allies had no intention of handing over anything so modern and powerful, but the Soviets did get a respectable set of Italian fleet units, which entered service in the Black Sea. Few gave active service past the mid-1950s.

Major units from Italy (+ those too damaged to restore)

> Battleship: 1
> Light cruiser: 1
> Destroyers: 2
> Torpedo boats: 3
> Submarines: 2 (+4)
> MTBs: 10
> Patrol cutters: 3
> Landing ships: 3
> Auxiliary ships: 19

Two views of Novorossiysk. *Her new owners understood both her superiority to other Soviet battleships and her limitations. A 1953 modernization fitted her with Soviet radars, fire control, and light AA guns.*

Novorossiysk *had an unfortunately short Soviet career, and her loss to a mine continues to generate conspiracy theories. Rather than try to restore an obsolescent dreadnought, the Soviets raised the wreck to remove the navigation hazard.*

Kerch, *the former Italian* Emanuele Filiberto Duca d'Aosta.

Destroyer Legkiy *(ex-*Fuciliere*). The potential for structural and sea-keeping problems in Italian ships was minimized by assigning them to the Black Sea Fleet.*

Two of Italy's more modern subs, Nichelio *and* Marea, *took the names* S-41 *and* S-42.

By far the biggest haul came from the German Navy. Negotiation with the Americans and British over proper allocations hit numerous sticking points. Germany's submarine fleet proved especially troublesome, with multiple dozens of hulls to account for. The final agreement handed each of the victors ten subs while 115 others were scuttled at sea, though in fact the Soviets had already swiped a number of damaged and incomplete U-boats (twenty out of Danzig harbor alone) prior to the negotiations. In the end, so many intact German vessels entered Soviet service that interest waned in units requiring extensive work.

Major units from Germany (+ those too damaged to restore)

> Light cruiser: 1
> Destroyers: 4
> Torpedo boats: 6
> Submarines: 10 (+24)
> Fleet minesweepers: 44
> Escort: 1
> MTBs: 30
> Motor minesweepers: 56
> Armed fishing cutters: 147
> Landing barges and lighters: 105

In addition, hundreds of auxiliary and non-combatant vessels transferred to the Soviets officially, to join numerous undocumented units and others already captured during the War. Soviet enthusiasm in seizing anything of potential value became a source of amusement to the Western Allies, though some items caused less amusement than others; the Soviets controlled the sunken remains of major warships, including a couple of elderly battleships and two heavy cruisers. Most prominently, the aircraft carrier *Graf Zeppelin* raised concern until the Soviets allowed an inspection of the wreck and agreed to dispose of her in short order.

German reparations arrived by 1947, and most warships served actively into the mid-1950s, lingering in auxiliary duties until disposal at the end of the decade. Many of the smaller ships transferred to civilian control and lasted well into the 1960s. Several auxiliary ships survive to this day.

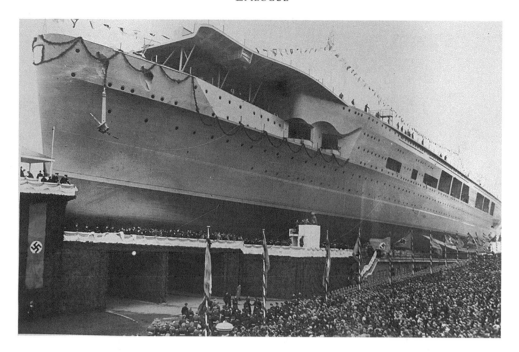

Launched with all due Germanic pomp, Graf Zeppelin *languished incomplete but gained a second chance when raised by the Soviets. Rumors of her accidental loss in Soviet custody thrived for decades though in fact the Soviets expended her as a target in accordance with their agreement. —author's collection.*

Tsel *(ex-Hessen) with the light cruiser* Admiral Makarov *(ex-Nürnberg) beyond. The Soviets recovered two pre-dreadnought battleships,* Hessen *and* Schleswig-Holstein; *such relics had little value except as targets.*

Sunk by bombs, the German cruiser Lützow (*ex-*Deutschland) *looked promising enough to the Soviets, who raised her but found her damage too extensive to warrant further effort.*

The large torpedo boat T 33 *before she became the Soviet* Primernyi. *—courtesy of WGAZ Marineschule Mürwik.*

Germany's S-boats ranked as the most capable MTBs of the war. —courtesy of WGAZ Marineschule Mürwik.

Appendix 1

ORDNANCE DATA

Guns

Bore/Length	Gun designation	Mount designation	Number of barrels	Rate of fire, rpm	Muzzle velocity, m/
406mm/50	B-37	MK-1	3	1.75-2.5*	830
356mm/52	Mod. 1913	Metal Factory	3	3*	731.5
305mm/54	B-50	MK-15	3	3.24*	900
305mm/52	Mod. 1907	MK-3-12 (MK-3-12mod)	3	1.8 (2.2)	762
180mm/60	B-1-K	MK-1-180	1	6	920
180mm/57	B-27	MK-3-180	3	5.5 [2**]	920
152mm/57	B-38	MK-5	3	7.5	950
152mm/50			1	4	823
130mm/50	B-13	B-13 (B-2-LM)	1 (2)	10 (12)	870
130mm/55	Mod. 1913	Obukhov	1	5-8	823
120mm/50	Mod 1905	Vickers (Obukhov)	1 (2)	7 (6.5)	825
102mm/60	Mod. 1911	Metal Factory (Obukhov)	1	12	823

* Theoretical ROF
** Practical ROF

Shell weight, kg	Max. range, m	Ceiling for AA guns, m	Ships
1108	46,300		*Sovetskiy Soyuz*
747.8	25,420		*Izmail*
470.9	48,152		*Kronshtadt*
470.9	23,520 (28,891)		*Sevastopol*
97.5	39,000		*Krasnyi Kavkaz*
97.5	37,040		*Kirov, Maxim Gorkiy*
55	28,520		*Chapaev, Sovetskiy Soyuz, Kronshtadt*
47.3	17,600		*Lenin* monitors
33.5	25,742		All modern destroyers (leaders, modern river monitors)
33.5	18,520		*Izmail, Avrora, Komintern, Svetlana*, sea-going gunboats, river monitors
26.3	14,075 (15,186)		*Sevastopol*, (*Lenin*)
17.5	16,300 (14,075)		WWI destroyers, *Uragan, Fugas*, old patrol ships and gunboats

102mm/45	B-2 (B-18)	B-2 (MK-2-4)	1 (2)	6-12	755
100mm/47	P	Minisini	2	12	880
100mm/51	B-24-PL	B-24-PL	1	12	872
100mm/56	B-24-BM	B-24-BM	1	12	900
100mm/56	B-34 (B-54)	B-34 (M3-14)	1	15 (16)	900
85mm/52	90-K	90-K (92-K)	1 (2)	15-18	800
76.2mm/55	34-K	34-K (39-K)	1 (2)	20	813
76.2mm/30	Lender	8-K	1	30	588
45mm/68	21-KM	21-KM	1	40	835
45mm/46	21-K	21-K (41-K)	1 (2)	25-30	760
37mm/67.5	70-K	70-K	1	150	880
25mm/83	84-KM	84-KM	1	200	910
12.7mm/79	DShK	DShK	1	250	850
7.62mm	Maxim	M-1 (M-4)	1 (4)	520	862

17.5	16,668		D, L, P submarines, (*Zheleznyakov*)
14	22,000	9800	*Krasnyi Kavkaz, Svetlana*
15.8	22,000		D, L, P, S, K class subs
15.8	23,335		*Uragan, Yastreb, Fugas*
15.8	22,000	10,000	*Kirov, Maxim Gorkiy, (Sovetskiy Soyuz, Kronshtadt)*
	15,500	10,500	*Yastreb, Maxim Gorkiy, Artillerist, Ognevoi*
6.61	14,600	9500	Most large and medium-sized ships
	11,000	6000	Older warships
1.41	10,600	6400	Small warships 1942 on
1.41	9500	6000	Most Soviet warships up to 1942
0.732	8400	5000	Most Soviet warships 1941 on
0.627	3000	3000	Small warships
0.052	3500	2400	Most Soviet warships
0.012	2400	1000	Most Soviet warships up to 1941

Torpedoes

Name	Size	Year	Total weight, kg	Explosive weight, kg
45-36-N	450mm	1936	935	200
45-36-NU	450mm	1939	1028	285
53-27 Type 1	533mm	1927	1675	200
53-27 Type 2	533mm	1927	1725	250
53-36	533mm	1936	1700	300
53-38	533mm	1938	1615	300
53-38U	533mm	1939	1725	400
53-39	533mm	1941	1800	317
EhT-80	533mm	1942	1800	400

Range: m at knots	Carried by
3000 at 41 6000 at 32	Surface ships
3000 at 41 6000 at 32	Surface ships
3700 at 43.5	Submarines, MTBs
3700 at 43.5	Submarines, MTBs
4000 at 43.5 8000 at 33	Surface ships, submarines, MTBs
4000 at 44.5 8000 at 34.5 10,000 at 30.5	Surface ships, submarines, MTBs
4000 at 44.5 8000 at 34.5 10,000 at 30.5	Surface ships, submarines, MTBs
4000 at 51 8000 at 39 10,000 at 34	Surface ships, submarines, MTBs
4000 at 29	Submarines

Mines

Name	Type	Total weight, kg	Explosive weight, kg
Model 1908	Moored mine	575	115
Model 1912	Moored mine	600	105
Model 1916	Moored mine	750	115
Model 1908/39	Moored mine	592	115
Model 1926	Moored mine	960	242-254
KB	Moored mine	1065	230
AG	Moored mine	1120	230
YaM	Moored mine	172	20
PLT(G)	Submarine moored mine	820	230
YhP(G)	Submarine moored mine	1050	300
PLT-2	Submarine moored mine	765	300
A-IV	Magnetic mine	671	330
A-V	Magnetic mine	455	280-290
AMD-500	Magnetic mine	500	300
AMD-1000	Magnetic mine	1000	700
R	River moored mine	190	8
R-1	River moored mine	275	40
MIRAB	River moored mine	280	64

Depth max./min., m	Max. deployment speed, knots
125/--	14
150/--	30
452/--	14
110/15	8
130/18	24
263/12	24
320/12	24
50/2.5	25
260/14.5	--
400/25	12
Unlimited/3	--
22/9	--
--/9	--
30/3	--
30/3	--
140/--	6
35/1.8	17-18
--/2	--

Appendix 2

MAJOR SUPPORTING UNITS

Monitors: major units, 1920-45; see page 220 for key

Class Name	Number of Units	Class Comm.	Displ., tons	Dimensions, m	HP	Speed, kn.
Lenin	7	1910	1100	71.0 x 12.8 x 1.6	2270	11.3
Udarnyi	1	1934	252.5	55.4 x 11.0 x 0.6	400	9
Aktivnyi	1	1935	314	50.7 x 8.2 x 1.1	480	8.5
Zheleznyakov	6	1936	263	51.2 x 8.2 x 0.9	280	8.5
Khasan	2	1942-43	1900	88.0 x 11.1 x 2.9	3200	15.4
Bobruisk [P]	4	1920	130	34.5 x 5.1 x 0.7	200	9
Smolensk [P]	1	1926	150	36.6 x 6.2 x 0.7	140	9
Berdyansk [R]	1	1904	650	59.0 x 9.5 x 1.6	1400	10
Azov [R]	2	1907	750	62.0 x 10.5 x 1.8	1800	13
Izmail [R]	1	1915	550	62.2 x 10.5 x 1.7	1600	12
Kerch [R]	1	1915	770	62.0 x 10.5 x 1.8	1600	12

Range, nm	Armament	Crew
10,745	Four 152mm, two 37mm, six 20mm, four 12.7mm mgs, five 7.62mm mgs	152
325	Two 130mm, two 45mm, four 7.62mm mgs	74
2750	Two 102mm, four 45mm, one 37mm, three 12.7mm	68
3700	Two 102mm, three 45mm, two 37mm, three 12.7mm	72
5920	Six 130mm, four 76.2mm, six 45mm, ten 12.7mm mgs, 29 mines	251
650	Three 76.2mm, four 7.62mm mgs	
650	Two 122mm, two 45mm, three 7.62mm mgs	36
550	Three 120mm, four 37mm, four 20mm, two 7.92mm mgs, one 7.62mm mg	129
830	Three 120mm, five 37mm, two 20mm, four 12.7mm, two 7.92mm	119
	Four 120mm, five 37mm, two 20mm, four 12.7mm, six 7.7mm mgs	125
500	Four 120mm, five 37mm, two 20mm, four 12.7mm mgs, one 7.92mm mg	133

Gunboats: major units, 1920-45

Class Name	Number of Units	Class Comm.	Displ., tons	Dimensions, m	HP	Speed, kn.
Krasnoe Znamya	1	1897	1823	72.2 x 12.7 x 4.0	2200	14.5
Bakinskiy Rabochiy	3	1905	760	73.2 x 7.2 x 3.6	6200	19
Buryat	2	1907	320	54.6 x 8.2 x 1.1	500	9.1
Krasnaya Zvezda	2	1908	338	54.5 x 8.2 x 1.2	480	10
Votyak	1	1908	383	54.6 x 8.3 x 1.3	500	10
Lenin	2	1910	750	61.6 x 8.6 x 2.8	2200	15
Pioner	1	1916	570	55.0 x 7.2 x 3.5	1500	14
El'pidifor	4	1920-23	1400	74.7 x 10.4 x 3.6	750	8
Trudovoy [P]	2	1933-38	32	18.1 x 4.6 x 0.34	120	6
Angara [R]	3	1916	375	60.2 x 6.9 x 2.0	900	12.6
KL-55 [J]	4	1934-35	568	59.4 x 8.8 x 0.9	680	13

Range, nm	Armament	Crew
1050	Five 130mm, seven 45mm, 50 mines	201
1300	Three 102mm, two 45mm, two 37mm, four 12.7mm mgs, two 7.62mm mgs	110
935	Two 76.2mm, two 37mm, seven 12.7mm, 80 mines	82
285	Two 100mm, three 37mm, five 12.7mm, 40 mines	81
285	One 100mm, one 76.2mm, four 7.62mm mgs, 80 mines	81
3100	Three 100mm, four 37mm, six 12.7mm, two 7.62mm, 30 mines	120
300	Two 102mm, one 37mm, 30 mines	52
2300	Three 130mm, two 76.2mm, two 45mm, two 37mm, five 12.7mm mgs, 180 mines	169
	Three 76.2mm, three 7.62mm mgs	51
3200	One 88mm, one 37mm, one 20mm, two 7.92mm mgs, two DC throwers	
	Three 120mm, six 12.7mm	

Patrol Ships: major units, 1920-45

Class Name	Number of Units	Class Comm.	Displ., tons	Dimensions, m	HP	Speed, kn.
Razvedchik	1	1905	185	36.0 x 4.8 x 2.3	300	12.5
Konstruktor	1	1906	820	60.5 x 8.2 x 3.3	8400	16
Atarbekov	3	1916	200	30.5 x 5.8 x 2.7	1600	14
Ametist	1	1916	250	52.0 x 5.3 x 2.9	3500	25
Uragan	18	1931-38	600	71.5 x 7.4 x 2.3	5700	21
Brilliant	4	1936-37	580	62.0 x 7.2 x 2.6	2200	17.2
Yastreb	2	1945	995	85.7 x 8.4 x 3.2	23,000	34
EK-1*	28	1943-44	2277	92.6 x 11.5 x 4.5	5500	19.4
Musson [R]	2	1914	262	58.0 x 5.8 x 1.5	5000	24

Range, nm	Armament	Crew
500	Two 45mm, two 7.62mm mgs	38
1000	Three 100mm, two 45mm, two 37mm, one 20mm, two 12.7mm mgs	105
	Two 76.2mm, two 7.62mm mgs	46
666	Three 45mm	42
930	Two 102mm, two 37mm, three 450mm torpedoes, two DC throwers, 20 mines	114
3500	One 102mm, two 45mm, one 37mm, two 12.7mm mgs, two DC racks, 31 mines	61
2800	Three 100mm, four 37mm, six 12.7mm, three 450mm torpedoes, 24 mines	177
9100	Three 76.2mm, two 40mm, nine 20mm, nine DC throwers, two DC racks	195
	Two 66mm, two mgs	30

Subchasers: major units, 1920-45

Class Name	Number of Units	Class Comm.	Displ., tons	Dimensions, m	HP	Speed, kn.
Nickson	1	1906	75	27.5 x 3.6 x 1.4	1700	16.5
BK-02	1	1934	75	26.9 x 4.0 x 1.9	2250	18
MO-1	1	1935	51.1	26.0 x 3.8 x 1.2	2250	14
MO-2	27	1935-36	50	26.2 x 3.9 x 1.5	2250	26
MO-3	4	1935	55.4	26.2 x 4.0 x 1.2	2065	24
MO-4	219 (+44) **	1937-44	56.5	26.9 x 4.0 x 1.5	2550	25.5
MO-5	1	1941	60	27.2 x 4.8 x 1.5	2550	26
Artillerist	23	1941-45	249	50.5 x 5.4 x 2	3600	22.3
MO-6	4	1943	66	26.8 x 4.0 x 1.4	3600	23
BMO (Pr.194)	66	1943-45	52.6	24.8 x 4.2 x 1.6	2400	21.2
OD-200	88	1943-45	47.2	23.4 x 4.0 x 1.8	1800	28
D-3 (PP-19-OK)	56	1943-44	38.9	22.1 x 4.0 x 1.7	2200	23.8
BO-2 (SC)*	78	1942-44	146	34.0 x 5.7 x 2.1	2400	18.6
R [G]	4	1943	140	36.6 x 5.8 x 2.1	1800	21.5
MO-851 [R]	3	WWII	60	26.0 x 6.0 x 2.7		8

Range, nm	Armament	Crew
600	Two 45mm, two 12.7mm mgs, two DC racks	21
285	Two 45mm, two 12.7mm mgs, two DC racks, four mines	20
400	Two 12.7mm mgs, two DC racks, four mines	21
285	Two 45mm, two 12.7mm mgs, two DC racks, four mines	21
	Two 45mm, two 12.7mm mgs, two DC racks	21
367	Two 45mm, two 12.7mm mgs, two DC racks, four mines	21
700	Two 45mm, two 12.7mm mgs, two DC racks	21
1300	One 85mm, two 37mm, two 12.7mm mgs, two DC throwers	49
700	Two 45mm, two 12.7mm mgs, two DC racks	23
495	One 37mm, five 12.7mm mgs	
590	One 37mm, one 25mm, two 12.7mm mgs, two DC racks	19
	One 37mm, two 12.7mm mgs	
2800	One 40mm, three 20mm, two DC throwers, one DC rack	33
1100	Two 45mm, two 37mm, one 12.7mm mg	37
	One 37mm, one 20mm	

Minelayers: major units, 1920-45

Class Name	Number of Units	Class Comm.	Displ., tons	Dimensions, m	HP	Speed, kn.
Narova	1	1877	4690	88.3 x 14.6 x 7.5	3300	12
Dunay	1	1892	1380	62.1 x 10.3 x 3.7	1500	10.5
Marti	1	1896	6189	122.3 x 15.4 x 7	11,426	14
Volga	1	1905	1710	71.3 x 11.8 x 4.4	1600	13
Okean	3	1936-37	3200	80.6 x 13.0 x 5.6	2400	13.4
Zyuyd	1	1937	860	56.8 x 9.3 x 3.0	600	11.1

Minesweepers: major units, 1920-45

Class Name	Number of Units	Class Comm.	Displ., tons	Dimensions, m	HP	Speed, kn.
Udarnik	3	1912-17	210	43.7 x 6.1 x 2.5	350	12
Virsaitis	2	1917	586	60.0 x 7.5 x 2.4	1850	16
Viesturs	2	1926	310	48.8 x 6.4 x 1.8	750	14.7
Fugas	40	1937-41	476	62.0 x 7.2 x 2.4	2800	18
Vladimir	2	1942-43	879	79.2 x 8.1 x 2.5	8000	22.4
AM*	34	1943	914.4	56.1 x 10.2 x 3.0	1800	15
YMS*	43	1942-44	330	41.5 x 7.5 x 2.6	1000	14.2
TAM*	7	1929-30	540	37.4 x 7.4 x 4.0	850	12
MMS*	5	1942	400	44.2 x 7.5 x 4.4	500	10.5
253-L	92	1944-45	108	36.0 x 5.1 x 1.3	690	12

	Range, nm	Armament	Crew
	2400	Two 75mm, two 47mm, two 7.62mm, 250 mines	145
	1000	One 76.2mm	59
	2260	Four 130mm, seven 76.2mm, three 45mm, three 12.7mm	390
	1650	Two 75mm, two 47mm, two 7.62mm mgs	121
	3600	Three 130mm, four 76.2mm, eight 7.62mm mgs, 158 mines	163
	5300	Two 76.2mm, six 45mm, two 20mm, two 12.7mm mgs, two	105

	Range, nm	Armament	Crew
	550	One 75mm, one 45mm, three 7.62mm, 36 mines	37
	2000	Three 102mm, four 37mm, two 12.7mm mgs	66
	672	One 76.2mm, one 45mm, one 20mm, three 12.7mm mgs	49
	2560	One 100mm, one 45mm, 31 mines	52
	2000	Two 100mm, one 45mm, three 37mm, two 20mm, four	125
	7050	One 76.2mm, two 40mm, six 20mm, two 7.62mm	95
	2000	One 76.2mm, two 20mm, three 12.7mm mgs, one 7.62mm	44
	2000	One 20mm, two 12.7mm mgs, two 7.62mm mgs	41
		Two 20mm, two 7.62mm mgs	31
	2400	Two 45mm, two 12.7mm mgs	21

MTBs: major units, 1920-45

Class Name	Number of Units	Class Comm.	Displ., tons	Dimensions, m	HP	Speed, kn.
ANT-3	1	1927	8.9	17.3 x 3.3 x 0.9	1200	54
ANT-4	1	1928	10	16.8 x 3.3 x 0.8	1200	50.5
Sh-4	59	1929-32	10	16.8 x 3.3 x 0.8	1200	50.5
Stal'noy	2	1931	28	23.5 x 3.8 x 1.4	2250	26
ANT-5	1	1933	14.5	19.1 x 3.4 x 1.2	2000	58
G-5	329	1934-44	17.8	19.1 x 3.3 x 1.2	2000	52
DTK	3	1937				
L-5	4	1939-40	11.3	24.0 x 5.4	2000	70
G-6	1	1939	86	36.5 x 6.6 x 1.9	7760	49.8
G-8	1	1940	31.3	24.2 x 3.8 x 1.5	4000	32
D-2	1	1940				
D-3	73	1940-44	36.1	22.4 x 4.0 x 1.9	2550	32
Komsomolets	32	1940-45	16.98	18.5 x 3.4 x 1.2	2400	51.6
SM-3	1	1941	34	20.8 x 3.9 x 1.5	3600	30
SM-4	1	1941	42	22.0 x 4.1 x 1.8	4000	30
L-9	3	1941	2.13			
STK-DD	1	1943	50	25.0 x 4.0	3000	34
Yunga (TM-200)	5	1945	46.9	23.4 x 4 x 1.7	3600	30.7

Range, nm	Armament	Crew
340	One 450mm torpedoes, two 7.62mm mgs, two mines	3
300	Two 450mm torpedoes, one 7.62mm mg, two mines	5
300	Two 450mm torpedoes, one 7.62mm mg, two mines	5
170	Three 450mm torpedoes, two 7.62mm mgs	6
	Two 533mm torpedoes, two 7.62mm mgs, four mines	6
220	Two 533mm torpedoes, one 7.62mm mg	6
250	Two 450mm torpedoes, two 12.7mm mgs	5
435	Three 533mm torpedoes, one 45mm, one 12.7mm mg, four 7.62mm mgs, three mines	30
350	Three 533mm torpedoes, three 12.7mm mgs, three mines	10
500	Two 533mm torpedoes, two 12.7mm mgs	9
650	Two 533mm torpedoes, one 12.7mm mg	7
380	Two 533mm torpedoes, two 12.7mm mg	8
	Three 12.7mm mgs	9
1000	Four 450mm torpedoes, three 12.7mm mgs, three mines	11
488	Two 533mm torpedoes, three 12.7mm mgs	11

A-1 (Vosper)*	83	1943-44	43.5	22.1 x 6.1 x 1.6	3600	39.3
A-2 (Higgins)*	52	1942-45	49	23.8 x 6.1 x 1.7	4050	36.3
A-3 (Elko) *	31	1944	51.1	24.5 x 6.3 x 1.5	3600	38.4
Lürssen [B]	3	1938-39	62	28.0 x 4.5 x 1.6	2850	33

Armored motor boats: major units, 1920-45

Class Name	Number of Units	Class Comm.	Displ., tons	Dimensions, m	HP	Speed, kn.
Kop'ye	2	1912	25	22.5 x 3.1 x 0.7	200	8.5
K	4	1914-17	31	20.4 x 3.2 x 1.1	800	14.7
N	3	1916	26.5	15.3 x 3.1 x 0.8	90	7
D	4	WWI	10	9.2 x 2.5 x 0.9	100	9
Partizan	2	1932	55.6	32.0 x 3.4 x 0.8	1600	17.3
1124	97	1936-45	52.2	25.3 x 4.1 x 0.9	1800	19.4
1125	151	1938-45	26.5	22.7 x 3.5 x 0.5	1770	19.7
S-40	7	1942	31.9	24.7 x 3.9 x 0.5	800	19
MBK (Pr.161)	20	1943-44	157.8	26.2 x 5.2 x 1.28	2400	13
MKL (Pr.186)	8	1945	156	36.2 x 5.2 x 1.5	1000	14
BK-125 [J]	6	1934-35	65	29.7 x 4 x 0.8	240	14
P [P]	17	1930's	13			10

Captured classes: [G] from Germany, [J] from Japan, [P] from Poland, [B] from Bulgaria, [R] from Romania

* Lend-Lease classes   ** NKVD ships

	450	Two 533mm torpedoes, one 20mm, four 12.7mm mgs, two mines	11
	420	Two 533mm torpedoes, two 20mm, four 12.7mm mgs, two mines	11
		Two 533mm torpedoes, one 40mm, one 20mm, four 12.7mm mgs, two mines	14
	880	Two 533mm torpedoes, one 20mm, two 15mm mgs	14

	Range, nm	Armament	Crew
	315	One 76.2mm, two 7.62mm mgs, 10 mines	12
	200	Two 76.2mm, two 7.62mm mgs, eight mines	14
	325	One 76.2mm, three 7.62mm mgs, six mines	8
	200	One 37mm, one 7.62mm mg, seven mines	7
	600	One 76.2mm, two 7.62mm mgs	13
	325	Two 76.2mm, two 12.7mm mgs, two 7.62mm mgs, 10 mines	17
	250	One 76.2mm, two 12.7mm mgs, one 7.62mm mgs	13
	125	One 76.2mm, three 76.2mm mgs	13
	450	Two 76.2mm, one 37mm, four 12.7mm mgs	38
	600	Two 85mm, one 37mm, four 12.7mm mgs	42
		Two 45mm, two 12.7mm mgs	
		One mg	

The world's first heavy icebreaker, Ermak *was designed by Russia's famous Admiral Makarov in the 1890s and built in England in 1899. Serving in the North, she had the misfortune to visit Leningrad for servicing in 1941, getting trapped there, yet she survived the war.*

Komintern *undergoing restoration in the 1920s with guns dismounted and the hull being primed and painted. The stern walk, an old tsarist feature, contrasts with the Communist star.*

Parizhskaya Kommuna *in 1924. Not every navy had to manage such conditions, with training and at-sea time cut by one third, but at least it made time for regular maintenance.*

The sense of prestige tied to Soviet icebreakers is apparent in the names for the "Leader" class. Iosef Stalin *in 1942 shows a mix of 100mm B-34 guns and Lend-Lease 20mm Oerlikons.* – courtesy of History on CD-ROM

Built as the stoker training ship, Okean Komsomolets *nearly achieved fame when nominated for conversion to an aircraft carrier in 1925, but the idea faded owing to the lack of financing.*

The Soviets never officially registered a hospital ship during World War II. Gruziya *served as a medical transport but was lost on 14 June 1942 while transporting ammo and troops to besieged Sevastopol.*

Gunnery practice aboard one of the Baltic battleships. Apart from their relative inefficiency, coal-fired boilers presented gunnery complications, so battleship modernization included oil-firing with boilers from the unfinished Izmail *class.*